COSA NOSTRA

MASSIMO PICOZZI

COSA NOSTRA

AN ILLUSTRATED HISTORY OF

THE MAFIA

PREFACE BY
CARLO LUCARELLI

WITH AN AFTERWORD BY
PIETRO GRASSO

W · W · NORTON

NEW YORK · LONDON

MONDADORI

To the victims of Mafia violence.
To those who have lost their lives opposing it and fighting it.
To the sorrow of those dear to them.
To those who, day after day, did not let up in the struggle.

Originally published in Italian in 2010 by
Mondadori Electa S.p.A
© 2012 Mondadori Electa S.p.A., Milano
English translation © 2012 Mondadori Electa S.p.A., Milano

Manufactured by Mondadori Printing, Verona

Library of Congress Cataloging-in-Publication Data

Picozzi, Massimo, 1956-
  [Cosa nostra. English]
  Cosa nostra : an illustrated history of the mafia / Massimo Picozzi.
      p. cm.
  "Originally published in Italian in 2010 by Mondadori Electa S.p.A."
  Includes bibliographical references and index.
  ISBN 978-0-393-34196-6 (pbk.)
  1. Mafia–History–Pictorial works. 2. Mafia–History. I. Title.
  HV6453.I83M374442513 2011
  364.106–dc23

                                2011041425

W. W. Norton & Company
500 Fifth Avenue, New York, NY 10110
www.wwnorton.com

W. W. Norton & Company Ltd.
Castle House, 75/76 Wells Street, London, WIT 3QT

1 2 3 4 5 6 7 8 9 0

Contents

6   **Nothing More Than Criminals**
Preface by Carlo Lucarelli

8   **Reasons for an Illustrated Book on the Mafia**
Introduction by Massimo Picozzi

10   **1. From Myth to Reality**
The Origins of the Cosa Nostra

24   **2. Gangs of New York**
Immigration, the Criminal Fringe,
and More

40   **3. United Italy Discovers the Mafia**
From the Notarbartolo Affair to
Benito Mussolini

50   **4. Senseless Prohibition**
The Golden Age of Mafia Gangsters

92   **5. An Obscure Period**
From the Landings in Sicily
to the Giuliano Enigma

122   **6. The Corleonesi Arrive**
Victims, Widows, and the
First Mafia War

138   **7. Lucky Luciano, Carlo Gambino,
and the Others**
Big Families and Big Bosses

178   **8. Corruption, Connivance, and Massacres**
From the Sack of Palermo to the Second
Mafia War

220   **9. The Buscetta Theorem**
The Season of the Maxi Trial

238   **10. The Last Godfathers**
The RICO Act, John Gotti, and the Decline

260   **11. From Massacres to Crisis**
The Attack on the State and the Response
from Institutions

280   **The Mafia Is Not Defeated**
Conclusion by Italy's National Anti-Mafia
Prosecutor Pietro Grasso

282   **Bibliography**

283   **Index of Names**

287   **Photo References**

Nothing More Than Criminals

Preface by Carlo Lucarelli

Many of them have earned a nickname, a sobriquet that sets them apart, such as Johnny "the Brain" Torrio or Carmine "the Snake" Persico. Things are much the same in Italy, with Bernardo Provenzano "'u Tratturi"—"the Tractor"—or Giovanni Brusca "lo Scannascristiani"—"the Mankiller," cristiani ("Christians") a stand-in for human beings in general.

On March 7, 2010, the first museum dedicated to the gangsters of the Cosa Nostra was opened, at 80 St. Mark's Place, in New York City. The $25 entrance fee includes a "mob tour," a three-hour tourist stroll through the streets of Little Italy. Among the spots visited are the places where Lucky Luciano and John Gotti lived or where filmmakers have shot such well-known films as *Donnie Brasco* and the second *Scarface*.

Asked why he thought the museum was a good idea—not on the ethical plane but in commercial terms—the museum's director Eric Ferrara responded that "historically, popular culture has always loved gangsters and all those figures who lived outside the boundaries of the system."

Up to that point we can agree with the enterprising Ferrara. The same is not true, however, of the second part of his statement, when he added, "I think the new interest is tied to the economic crisis, to the fact that we no longer have control of our lives and we fantasize about anyone who, for good or for bad, seems to have managed to take control of his destiny."

The economic crisis may have very little to do with it, for the fascination of the Cosa Nostra has roots deeply embedded in a concept that has remained undiminished in spite of its having been contradicted time and again by wretched and cowardly reality.

Nearly 150 years have passed since the first appearance of the term *mafia* in a written document. In 1863, Giuseppe Rizzotto and Gaetano Mosca got together to compose a theatrical work they titled *I mafiusi di la Vicaria*, Vicaria being Palermo's prison. And the imprisoned *mafiusi* are depicted as men who have experienced misfortune but maintain a profound sense of morality, men who are always ready to protect the weak from the powerful and do so even from behind bars.

Two years later Giuseppe Pitré, Italy's famous scholar of folklore, who liked to call himself a professor of "folk psychology," wrote that the Mafia "is neither a sect nor an association, it does not have regulations or statutes . . . The mafioso is not a thief, not a criminal . . . The Mafia is the consciousness of one's own being, the exaggerated concept of one's individual strength, the only arbiter of every conflict of interests or ideas. . . . The mafioso is someone who always wants to give and receive respect. If someone offends him, he does not turn to the law."

It may seem strange that a scholar should have such a benevolent concept of the Mafia, but even more surprising is that the concept of the *mafioso* as a man of honor, above the law yet following laws of his own, fair with the weak but merciless with the powerful, endured without suffering so much as a dent until the arrival of Tommaso Buscetta. Only since 1984, by way of the testimony rendered to Judge Falcone, have we begun to understand the structure of the Cosa Nostra, the direction of its power, its use of violence and murder.

This situation of culpable blindness was not restricted to Italy, for in the United States the omnipotent J. Edgar Hoover, director of the FBI for nearly fifty years, had steadfastly refused to believe in the existence of a criminal organization called the "Mafia."

Collusion or mere shortsightedness?

The most ordinary of news reports have kept us from losing time in doubt, given that criminal alliances among the Mafia, politics, and the business world go on under the eyes of everyone.

In describing the terrible period of the ascent to power of the Corleonesi, the time known as *la mattanza*[1] ("the killing"), I used these words : "There are stories that seem like novels, even films . . . novels to read in one sitting, films to see and remember scene by scene . . . Only you can't do that with these stories, you can't remember them with satisfaction the way you can with made-up adventure stories. Because they're ugly stories and because they're true stories."

The design of this book, the way it reviews events and figures by way of photographic documentation and including space dedicated to the victims, illuminates how much the story of the Mafia is an ugly story.

The book makes clear how behind people such as Lucky Luciano or Totò Riina, John Gotti and Bernardo Provenzano and Giovanni Brusca there is no merit whatsoever, and nothing at all to fantasize about. With all due respect to Eric Ferrara.

Instead, all the courage can be read in the faces and the bodies of those who, confronted with violence, intimidation, and extortion, chose not to give in, a decision for which they paid with their lives.

[1] Carlo Lucarelli, *La Mattanza*, 2004.

Reasons for an Illustrated Book on the Mafia

Introduction by Massimo Picozzi

September 29, 1984, has gone down in history as the day of the San Michele blitz. On the basis of the revelations of Tommaso Buscetta, 366 arrest warrants were issued covering an unsettling number of crimes, among them 121 murders. On that Saturday, in a single night, entire Mafia clans were transferred to seven maximum-security Italian prisons.

On the night of the San Michele blitz I myself, as a young doctor responsible for seeing to the health of the prisoners, was in one of those seven prisons. I had seen and heard many things over a year of service, but the chilling politeness of the new arrivals has been forever impressed on my memory.

There was one prisoner in particular—giving his name here would be neither suitable nor meaningful—whose words I still remember: "Doctor, I trust you. I know you'll decide for the best." The subject of the conversation was a prescription for a pain reliever, or perhaps a sleeping pill, nothing vital. But the tone of voice and the gestures that accompanied his statement were the same as those I encountered two years later from Michele Greco, the "Pope," when at the end of the Maxi trial, and before the court withdrew to the chamber, he requested a microphone so he could say, in tones and cadences of a calm warning, "Signor Judge, I would like to wish you peace . . . because peace is tranquillity of the spirit, the conscience. And for the duty that awaits you, serenity is the foundation on which to judge. These aren't my words, they're the words of our lord who commanded Moses: 'When you must judge, decide with utmost serenity.' And I wish, Signor Judge, that this peace accompanies you for the rest of your life."

I spent a few more years working in a prison institute, but the experiences I had, actual and dramatic, have stayed with me for all my life. Because when you have to help judges and policemen investigate a murder case, or work up a profile, interrogate, write up psychiatrist's reports, you must count on what you know, rather than on what others have said or written.

By coincidence, with a specialty in psychiatry, I found myself on duty in the mental illness department of a public hospital on May 23 and then on July 19, 1992, the days on which the Mafia killed Falcone and Borsellino.

Working on this book was anything but easy.

The intention was never that of writing a manual on the history of the Cosa Nostra, with its Sicilian and American branches. Those seeking to investigate the subject can find thick volumes written by researchers who have dedicated their lives to this history. Or they can read the reports of journalists, investigators, and judges who have encountered the affairs of the Mafia because they have fought against them daily (to that end I allowed myself to add suggestions at the end of the volume in a brief bibliography).

It was not easy because the intention was to bring to life events and people by way of images, accompanying them with captions rich enough to provide information but not so important as to predominate.

The first, purely objective difficulty was that of selecting the images. Because of their function and value as documents, their significance and ability to transmit emotions and information, I labored to do without dozens of images. Had I not, the result would have been not an accessible volume but instead a volume of the thickness of a high school textbook.

The second problem was that of giving the text a narrative rhythm, with figures able to span different historical periods, and to make the story take place on the shores of the Mediterranean as well as on the other side of the Atlantic. Hence the decision to alternate chapters dedicated to Italian events with those on the American setting, with the inevitable crossovers.

Up to now I've discussed the difficulties of making this book; now come the decisions.

The first was never to indulge in the morbid.

The photos that present the victims of lethal acts were chosen not for shock value but because they are important in achieving an understanding. Special attention was given those who fell fighting the Mafia or those who had nothing to do with the battle but ended up dead all the same. There are snapshots that capture moments of tension but also of serenity, such as those in which Carlo Alberto Dalla Chiesa and Giovanni Falcone are seen radiant alongside their companions or the shot of the young Giuseppe Di Matteo on a beach during a vacation. Indeed, Cosa Nostra is meant primarily to be their story.

A final note. During the busy months dedicated to researching, selecting, documenting, and writing, along with the history books I consulted I had the good fortune to discover a short treatise by Vilèm Flusser titled *Towards a Philosopy of Photography*. The Czech philosopher, a psychiatrist frequently obliged to confront the semantics of madness, the intricate symbology of delirium, opened a new world to me. I am indebted to him for my decision to tell the history of the Mafia by means of photographs, so I will present here a passage from his small manual.

The significance of images is on the surface. One can take them in at a single glance yet this remains superficial. If one wishes to deepen the significance, i.e., to reconstruct the abstracted dimensions, one has to allow one's gaze to wander over the surface feeling the way as one goes. This wandering over the surface of the image is called "scanning." In doing so, one's gaze follows a complete path formed, on the one hand, by the structure of the image and, on the other, by the observer's intentions. The significance of the image as revealed in the process of scanning therefore represents a synthesis of two intentions: one manifested in the image and the other belonging to the observer. It follows that images are not "denotative" (unambiguous) complexes of symbols (like numbers, for example) but "connotative" (ambiguous) complexes of symbols. They provide space for interpretation.

To you then, and to your interpretations.

1 From Myth to Reality

The Origins of the Cosa Nostra

At the lowest level were the *picciotti*, foot soldiers in a criminal army; over every ten of them was a *capodecina* ("head of ten"). That unit can be taken as the building block for a hierarchical structure composed of a certain number of these groups of ten united to form a family, or *cosca*, usually known by the name of the city district in which it was active, the zone in which it exercised its control.

The *capo* ("boss"), or family representative, was supported by a *vicecapo* ("underboss") and a *consigliere* ("counselor"), of which each family was permitted no more than three. Several families in nearby territories, usually three, formed a *mandamento* ("district"), and the leader of each mandamento, known as a *capo-mandamento*, served as the representative of the families in the *cupola*, the directing organ of which was a *commissione*.

For many years the provincial commission of Palermo constituted the summit of this organization, but with the spread of the Mafia phenomenon to other cities in Sicily a regional cupola came into being.

This complex organization was regulated by ironclad laws that were part of an unwritten code that was, however, perfectly known to its members. There are those who believe this system was inspired by the ecclesiastical hierarchy, with its rituals and secrets. The comparison may be slightly exaggerated but the organization was most certainly secret and remained so until the courageous judge, Giovanni Falcone, began to dig, doing so with the collaboration of the first *pentiti*—"repentant" mafiosi who turned state's evidence—first among them Tommaso Buscetta.

We're talking about the Mafia, a criminal structure unique in the world, a state within the state, a deadly parasite that for more than a century proved itself capable of convincing everyone that its very existence was no more than the fruit of cultural stereotypes or was at most a political invention of the government in Rome.

Mafia: there is not even agreement on the origin of the term.

One theory, given scant credence, traces its derivation to the Arabic word *mahyas*, translatable as "arrogant boldness." There is then the evocative but also undocumented notion that "Mafia" is an acronym for *Mazzini autorizza furti incendi e avvelenamenti* ("Mazzini authorizes thefts, fires, poisonings"), coined in 1860 after the great Italian patriot took a mysterious trip to Sicily. Other sources hold that the word is from the Tuscan or Trentino dialects or even from that of the Veneto.

In fact, the first to speak of "brotherhoods and types of sects" dedicated to corruption and crimes was Pietro Calà Ulloa, a judge at Trapani, in a document that bears the date August 3, 1938.

The term made its first official appearance in a theatrical work written by Giuseppe Rizzotto and Gaetano Mosca in 1863. *I mafiusi di la Vicari* narrates the deeds of a group of prisoners in Palermo's Vicaria prison, today known as the Ucciardone. Two years later, the prefect of Palermo, Filippo Antonio Gualterio, in an official report associated the Mafia with the concept of a criminal organization.

In 1876 two scholar friends, Leopoldo Franchetti and Sidney Sonnino, went to Sicily to do research on the living conditions on the island; their investigation represents the first thorough document on the local political and administrative situation.

On May 11, 1860, Garibaldi landed at Marsala with his Thousand and, three days later, at Salemi, he declared he was taking possession of the island in the name of Victor Emanuel II.

While the great landowners looked upon this undertaking with little concern, convinced the new order would in no way compromise their interests, the peasants who gathered around Garibaldi believed the fall of the Bourbons would lead to greater justice accompanied by a redistribution of the land. They soon faced bitter disillusionment. Indeed, it can be affirmed that the bloody repression of the uprisings at Bronte—a town northwest of Etna where the peasants revolted in the hope of obtaining immediate relief for their terrible condition—marks the beginning of the phenomenon known as brigandage, often dismissed as a manifestation of delinquency, but in reality a form of protest and resistance that was hardly criminal, at least not in its intentions.

On March 17, 1861, Victor Emanuel II was proclaimed king of Italy, but the Savoy soon encountered the difficulties of ruling a territory so different from their own, both culturally and politically.

With their characteristic ability to seize and exploit the moment, the Mafia families presented themselves as allies for both the king and the big landowners. The landowners, ensconced in their splendid city homes, in order to draw the greatest profits entrusted their land to *gabellotti* (tenant farmers), who in turn exploited the labor of the peasants.

The gabellotti also depended on support from the Mafia to suppress the protests of the workers, but this discontent grew over the years and finally led to an organized movement, that of the Fasci Siciliani di Lavoratori, Sicilian Workers' Leagues.

From 1891 to 1894 groups of peasants were united in the struggle against the landowners, led by such highly charismatic figures as Giuseppe De Felice Giuffrida and Bernardino Verro. Before being liquidated by the bloody repression perpetrated by the army sent by Prime Minister Francesco Crispi, the leagues suffered attempts at infiltration by the Mafia; this was done not to destroy the leagues but rather with the intention of controlling from within a movement that could have become victorious. The Mafia has never followed the political views or interests of a single party but has instead made alliances with whomever at the moment enjoyed the most power.

With the suppression of the leagues, and the imprisonment of its leaders, the Mafia firmly aligned itself with the government, taking steps to sweep away any awkward or embarrassing situations, such as, for example, the awkward fate of Bernardino Verro, murdered while leaving the town hall of Corleone early on the afternoon of November 3, 1915.

1-2. The legend of the Beati Paoli, a secret brotherhood devoted to righting the wrongs committed by the powerful against the weak (opposite, filming a scene of puppet theater; right, poster still used today in street performances), came into being in the distant past. The earliest signs of it date to 1185, with the sect of the Vendicosi, the "Avengers," of whom the Beati Paoli were said to be an evolution, active in Palermo in the fifteenth and sixteenth centuries. According to Francesco Maria Emanuele e Gaetani, marchese of Villabianca, in a document written in the late eighteenth century, the sect opposed injustices committed by the nobles, met at night in secret locales, and organized itself into a law court. In December 1836 Vincenzo Linares repeated the legend in the pages of the Palermo periodical *Il Vapore*, but it was Luigi Natoli, in 1909, who gave the sect new fame with a popular novel that ran as a serial offered to readers of *Il Giornale di Sicilia*.

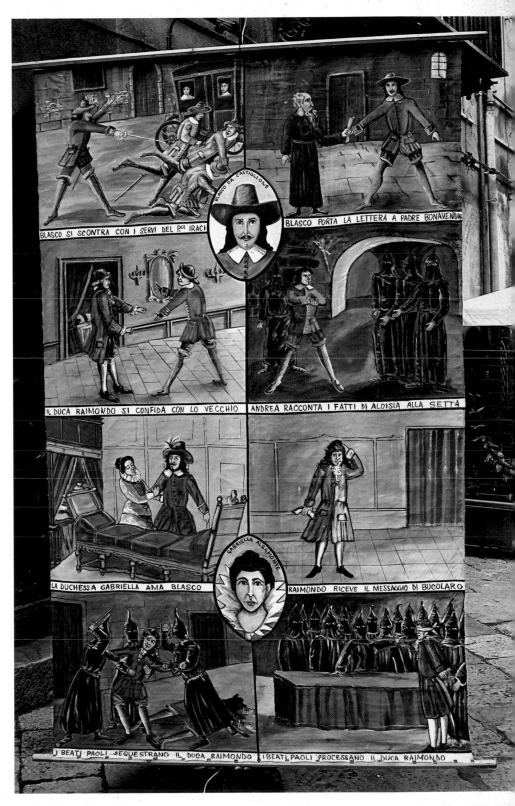

3. The Sicilian Vespers, in a painting by Francesco Hayez of 1846 preserved in the Galleria Nazionale d'Arte Moderna in Rome, was an event of great importance to the island's history. The rebellion took place in the thirteenth century, during the reign of the hated King Charles of Anjou, son of King Louis VIII of France. The revolt began at the hour of the sunset prayer of vespers on March 31, 1282, in the yard of the Church of the Holy Spirit in Palermo. A French soldier named Drouet made advances to a Sicilian woman accompanied by her husband. He grabbed away the soldier's sword and stabbed him with it, killing him. Over the centuries this incident has been cited as proof of the Sicilian code of honor, coming to be compared with the figure of the mafioso, understood as a daring man ready to respond to any act of injustice.

4. Enrico Caruso (1873–1921), in the role of Turiddu in an 1895 performance of the *Cavalleria Rusticana*. The one-act opera, composed by Pietro Mascagni (1863–1945), is centered on the love triangle of Alfio, Turiddu, and Lola and on the duel between the two men. The work, based on a story by Giovanni Verga, was performed in Rome in 1890 and was immediately taken on a tour of the large cities of the United States. The offstage exclamation "They have murdered Turiddu!" entered the collective imagination, along with the stereotype of the passionate Sicilian willing to face death to save his honor. When he composed the work Mascagni had never visited Sicily.

5. From *Il Giornale di Sicilia*, August 24, 1878, in an article about Vincenzo Capraro's gang: "Capraro was from Sciacca, but his fourteen men were from Sambuca, Contessa, Giuliana, Santa Margherita, and Castronuovo, communes located on the border between the province of Girgenti and that of Palermo. None of these men was from Sciacca. Between 1868 and 1878 the Capraro gang committed innumerable robberies, ravages, murders, armed revolts, extortions, and kidnappings; the principal crimes, those reported and known, numbered no fewer than thirty-eight, and among them were no fewer than nine kidnappings." To the right are portraits of two members of the gang, Filippo Merlo (who, despite the newspaper story, was originally from Sciacca) and Giuseppe Petralia, a native of Giuliana.

Capibanda siciliani

Antonino Leone
da Ventimiglia (Termini Imerese)

Placido Rinaldi
da S. Mauro Castelverde

6. These images of brigand chiefs Antonino Leone and Placido Rinaldi, positioned after death in poses for photographs, were preserved in the album of an old police official. Rinaldi, a native of Casteldilucio, was the leader of the Maurina gang, which was active in the countryside between Messina and Catania; the bounty on his head had reached 4,000 lire. He led the famous attack on the estate of the baroness Ciancio, making off with the incredible sum of 300,000 lire. On September 14, 1892, the commander of the *carabinieri* of the Pettineo Post, Vincenzo Venturi, along with his colleagues Francesco Navetta, Calogero Letizia, and Giovanni Castrogiovanni, while patrolling the Loreto district ran into the Maurina gang. In the shoot-out Rinaldi received a mortal wound.

7. Giuseppe Garibaldi (1807–1882) in a well-known photograph that displays the wounds to his thigh and foot received on August 29, 1862, on a mountain in Aspromonte. Garibaldi had been shot in a battle between his Redshirts and *bersaglieri* sent by the Italian government to keep him from completing his march on Rome, with the consequent driving out of the pope. Only two years earlier, on May 11, Garibaldi, at the head of the expedition of the Thousand, had landed at Marsala to the enthusiastic welcome of the Sicilians.

8–9. Sidney Sonnino (1847–1922; left), future president of the cabinet, arrived in Palermo on March 1, 1876, together with his friend Leopoldo Franchetti (1847–1917; above), with the aim of carrying out research, later published with as *Political and Administrative Conditions of Sicily*. The work, the first to confront the problem of the Mafia, awakened conflicting responses but without doubt it was an exceptional document. Franchetti, who began his career in parliament in 1882, was unable to stand the drama of the Italian defeat at Caporetto and took his life in Rome on November 4, 1917.

10. Taken around 1900, this photograph shows a group of peasants posed for the occasion dressed in their best outfits. They worked for the Lo Zocco farm company, which Louis-Philippe-Robert, duke of Orléans (first row, third from left), explorer, and pretender to the throne of France, possessed near Palermo. With rare exceptions it is difficult to make out so much as the hint of a smile on the faces of these workers, and indeed the living conditions of peasants between the end of the nineteenth century and the dawn of the twentieth were extremely harsh. An idea of what conditions were like can be gleaned from the stories of Giovanni Verga in *Life in the Fields* (1880), the same collection that included the *Cavalleria rusticana*.

11. The engraving opposite depicts the peasant league's attack on the magistrate's court and the fire of the customs tollhouses in January 1894. The movement, with its democratic and socialistic inspiration, grew in Sicily between 1891 and 1893, in the wake of peasant discontent but also as a result of unrest among the workers in sulfur mines, subjected to exhausting labor under unbearable conditions. The protest, which included strikes and violent clashes, reached its height in the summer of 1893, with the request for new rules in the renewal of rent contracts and sharecropping. To protect its interests, the ruling class called on the government of Prime Minister Francesco Crispi to intervene and an army was sent to dissolve the organization and arrest its leaders.

12. Bernardino Verro (1866–1915) had a simple, easy-to-understand lesson: a single rod is easy to break, breaking two requires more effort, but with an entire bundle it becomes impossible. It was essential for the workers to understand that if they put themselves together they'd have nothing more to fear from their employer. He shouted this lesson to peasants in September of 1892, founding the Corleone section of the Sicilian Leagues, one of the first in Sicily. His struggle to achieve, on July 1, 1893, the so-called Pacts of Corleone, the first trade-union contract in united Italy, was of fundamental importance. The cancellation of the leagues and the repression under Crispi condemned him to long imprisonment. Having served his time he was elected the first socialist mayor of Corleone, and he never quit battling injustices and the Mafia, which ordered his murder on November 3, 1915.

2 Gangs of New York

Immigration, the Criminal Fringe, and More

Gangs of New York, the popular 2002 film directed by Martin Scorsese, was liberally inspired by a work of that name published in 1927 by Herbert Asbury. Asbury's book is a milestone in the history of true crime, the literary genre in which facts and personages from the world of crime are presented in a novelistic style. The book, along with other sources, presents an illuminating image of New York City in the nineteenth and early twentieth centuries. For example, between 1880 and 1900 the number of Italian immigrants in New York rose enormously, from 20,000 to more than 250,000. In 1910, adding in the first-generation of Italian Americans, the number reached about 500,000.

Eighty percent of these Italians arrived from areas in southern Italy, and while the Sicilians established themselves along the East River, between 106th and 116th streets, the Neapolitans colonized Brooklyn and the East Side of downtown Manhattan, where they concentrated in the area of Mulberry Street in living conditions that were often miserable.

There is the story of an area of Mulberry Street known as the Mulberry Bend, site of a tumbledown rooming house, a block of apartments with 132 rooms. Health inspectors sent by the city discovered that fully 1,324 Italian immigrants lived in the building, crammed into the rooms by the dozen.

New Yorkers looked upon the Italians with a decidedly ambivalent attitude: on the one hand, the well-to-do loved to visit Italian restaurants and taste Italian food and wine, to have a personal barber from Italy, and to listen to bel canto and opera. Indeed, Enrico Caruso was a legend at the Metropolitan, founded in April 1880. On the other hand, there was the tendency to identify all immigrants with the narrow criminal fringe that inevitably accompanied them, and the New York City police, composed in large part of Irish immigrants, did nothing to prove the baselessness of the prejudice. To them, the Italians were hardly trustworthy people. They called all of them Pasquale, but all things considered the police didn't bother about the Italians provided they stayed within the borders of the areas they occupied. If they chose to tear one another apart, it hardly mattered.

Even so, the New York City Police Department often found the Italians' habits and ways of going about things disconcerting, as is well documented by a certain story. The leading figure in this story is the legendary detective Thomas F. Byrnes, an investigator of Irish origin comparable in terms of fame and talent to his French counterpart Eugène François Vidocq; other leading players include a group of Italians, among them Antonio Flaccomio, his friend Antonio Polazzi, and the brothers Carlo and Vincenzo Quarterano.

On the evening of October 14, 1888, the Quarteranos invited the other two men to dinner in a restaurant between Third Avenue and St. Mark's Square. In truth, their intentions were anything but friendly, since Polazzi had betrayed them, speaking too much to the wrong person. Polazzi, however, caught on to the danger in time to flee and save himself, leaving only Flaccomio, who tried to free himself from the wrath of the Quarteranos but received a good number of knife wounds and ended up bleeding to death on the sidewalk.

In charge of the investigation, Byrnes quite willingly gave an interview to the *New York Times* in which he explained that the Sicilians had formed a gang called the *Mafia*, that for them killing was only a kind of hobby, and if a member of the gang commited a serious crime in the city he immediately escaped capture by fleeing to his country of origin, and vice versa.

Byrnes found himself in difficulty dealing with people like the Quarteranos; his usual methods, based on the use of spies and informers infiltrating the underworld, along with rough interrogation methods, didn't get results with Italians.

Indeed, it even happened during that period that a young man was killed, hit by a bullet on the streets of Manhattan, and that an elderly man who witnessed the event, when interrogated, claimed to know nothing and not to know anyone involved, not the attackers, not the victim. All this only to discover a few hours later that the murdered man was none other than the elderly man's son.

So it was that the American police ran up against the code of silence, *omertà*, a word derived from "humility," meaning showing respect for one's superiors by cultivating the virtue of reserve.

At the end of the investigation Inspector Byrnes was categorical: never again would he become involved in a crime committed by Italians against other Italians. He unburdened himself with journalists: "Let them kill each other." He did not yet know that New York, the city he loved and that had welcomed him when he was still a baby, was about the receive a visit from a criminal figure of quite another character.

In 1889 Ignazio "the Wolf" Saietta arrived in the United States, fleeing a conviction for a murder he'd committed in his native city, Corleone. He was greeted by Giuseppe Morello, who had arrived a few years earlier for the same reasons, and with him were the Terranova brothers, Antonio, Vincenzo, and Ciro. The Wolf and Morello were to be in the forefront of crime during the first twenty years of the 1900s, once they had gotten past the risk of being taken out of circulation by the investigations into the crime that has passed into history as the Barrel Murder case. This took place in 1903, when a certain Benedetto Madonia was barbarously murdered, guilty of having meddled with the interests of Don Vito Cascio Ferro. The affair, presented in dramatic tones by the press, was immediately brought into perspective by a settling of accounts among mafiosi and was assigned to the Italian-American detective Joe Petrosino.

Petrosino got to the bottom of things brilliantly; too bad that between legalistic quibbling and witnesses who disappeared or suffered belated amnesia Madonia's killers ended up escaping justice.

Petrosino himself was killed in Palermo in March 1909, during a trip in which he proposed exposing the criminal traffic between the land of his forefathers and his adopted homeland. At news of the murder, President Theodore Roosevelt declared that the detective "was a great man, a good man. I knew him for years, and he did not know the name of fear."

This posthumous declaration was futile and paradoxical, like all the many others that governments and officials have thrown to the wind in the long history of the struggle against the Mafia.

1. Shown here are portraits of several members of the Matranga gang, active at the end of the nineteenth century. Charles Matranga was born in Sicily in 1857 and arrived in the United States when still a child. His family settled in New Orleans and, beginning in the 1870s, he became the leader of a criminal gang that controlled the commerce of citrus fruits along with the prostitution business and rackets. The easy earnings attracted the attention of the family of Joe Provenzano, resulting in the first Mafia war in American history, in which the chief of the New Orleans police, David Hennessey, also lost his life. Following investigations nineteen people were arrested and put in jail. On March 14, 1891, before a trial could take place, a furious crowd attacked the jail and lynched eleven of the prisoners, among them Joseph P. Macheca.

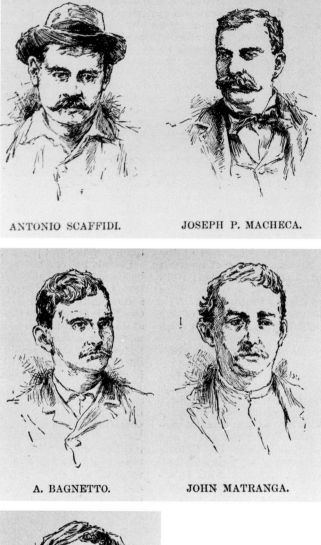

ANTONIO SCAFFIDI.   JOSEPH P. MACHECA.

A. BAGNETTO.   JOHN MATRANGA.

PIETRO MASTERO.

2. Lower Manhattan, New York City. The Five Points, shown here in an 1855 engraving, was among the city's poorest and most ill-famed neighborhoods. It took its name from the five corners created by the intersection of five streets: Cross, Orange, Anthony, Little Water, and Mulberry (the only one still bearing its original name). Beginning in 1870 the zone was occupied by a wave of immigrants, primarily Italians and Jews; the criminal fringe organized gangs that fought among themselves as well as with the Irish gangs already present in the area. Several gangs stood out because of their brutality, among them the Irish Whyos, the Jewish Monk Eastman Gang, and the Five Points gang of Paul Kelly, whose real name was Antonio Vaccarelli, a Sicilian who'd arrived around 1890. The ranks of the Five Points gang were to produce such figures as Frankie Yale, Johnny Torrio, Al Capone, Meyer Lansky, Bugsy Siegel, and Lucky Luciano.

3. Mulberry Street, shown here in an image taken around 1900, was the heart of Little Italy, running the length of that neighborhood from end to end. Always crowded with passersby, its sidewalks were invaded by peddlers with carts displaying their wares who competed with local shops. There were restaurants as well as banks in which immigrants deposited their earnings. Every September, Mulberry Street was closed to traffic for the San Gennaro Festival, an opportunity to watch games and performances and to sample sausages and zeppole, a typical sweet from southern Italy.

4. The immigrants who left Italy at the end of the nineteenth century believed America to be the promised land, a country where misery would be forgotten and a happy future could be built for oneself and one's children. The dream did not come true for everyone, as indicated by this photograph taken by Jacob Riis in 1888. Three sleeping homeless boys lie heaped in a corner of a church on Mulberry Street, waiting to beg a few pennies of charity at the conclusion of religious services. For youths like these, association with local criminals often represented the only means of survival. And those who survived were likely to be the most cynical and cruel.

5. Bandit's Roost was an alley off Mulberry Street. This photograph, taken in 1888 by Jacob Riis, shows the members of a gang glaring back at the camera with an air of challenge. Born in Denmark, Riis immigrated to the United States in 1870, at the age of twenty-one; he made a name for himself not so much as a journalist as for his work as a renowned documentary photographer. Impressed by Charles Dickens's descriptions of the slums of London, he collected his photographs in a book published in December 1889 called *How the Other Half Lives*, the "other half" being the poor, the homeless, the outcast. Riis won for himself a place of honor among the pioneers of photojournalism.

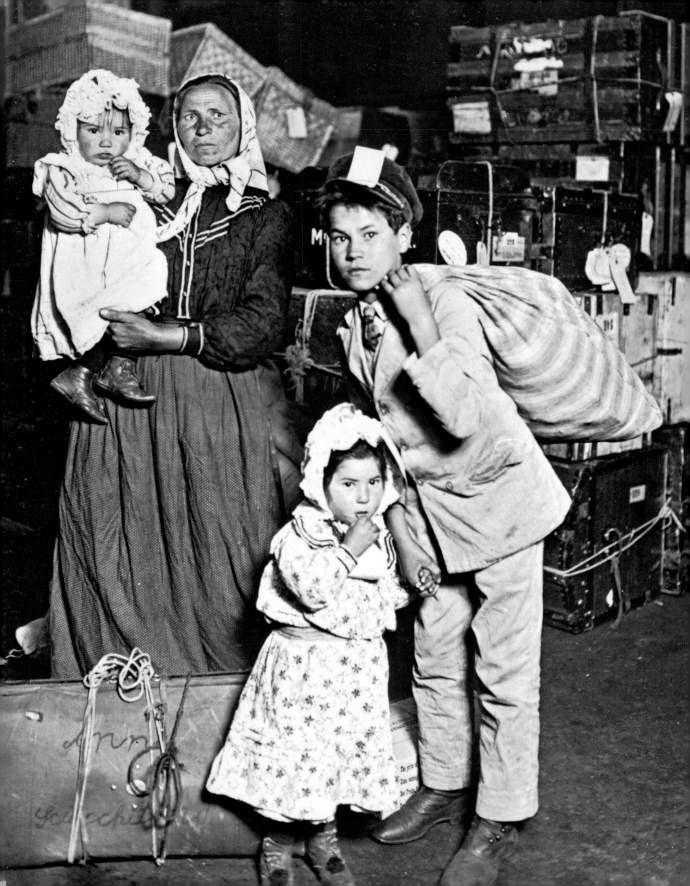

6. Her face marked by hardship, this woman has just arrived at Ellis Island, in 1905, with her three children. Behind them are the suitcases and trunks of other immigrants who, like them, have left behind family and friends to flee poverty. Ellis Island is a small island in the New York harbor. Beginning in 1892 it was the first stop for every immigrant, where identification was recorded, including profession and any criminal record; there was also a physical examination. The selection process was not overly rigid, given that only 2 percent of the new arrivals were sent back home, usually aboard the same ship on which they'd arrived. No fewer than 12 million immigrants are thought to have passed through Ellis Island, with a peak of more than 1 million in 1907.

7. October 24, 1919, and from the deck of a ship a girl points out something to the young girl at her side. Their long journey from Italy is about to end, and perhaps they can already make out the first skyscrapers of New York, such as the Woolworth Building, 800 feet high, inaugurated on April 24 six years earlier. For many, the ocean crossing was the first time they'd traveled far from their birthplace, and until the Italian government took control of immigration, in 1901, licensing carriers and inspecting facilities, the trip could be a dramatic experience in confined quarters with precarious hygienic conditions. Epidemic diseases frequently spread among the immigrants, with the youngest and the oldest those most likely to die.

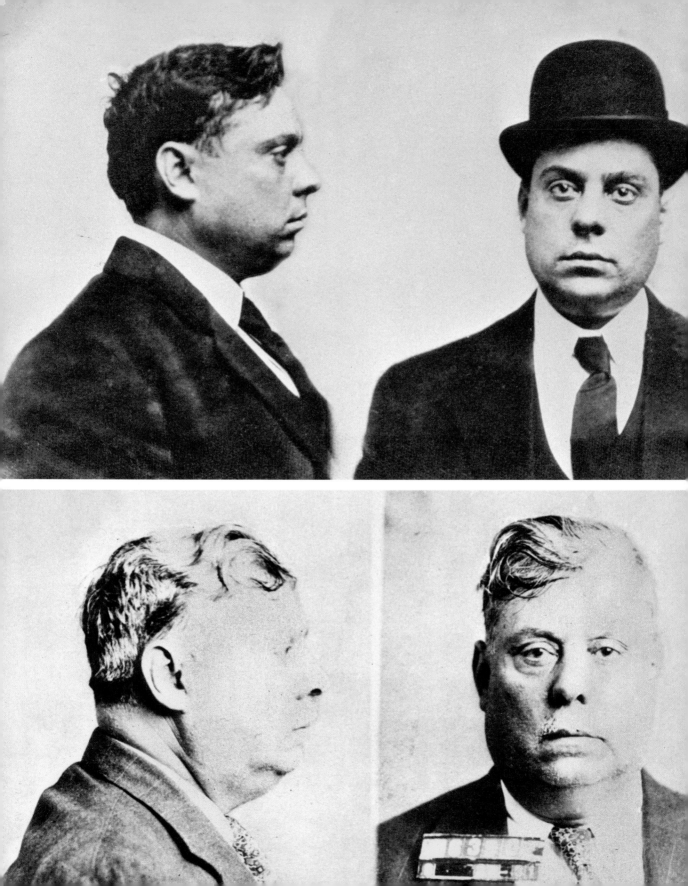

8–9. Ignazio Saietta, shown opposite in two pairs of identification photographs taken in 1909 and in 1936, was born in Corleone in 1877 and, at the age of twenty-one, was forced to flee Italy, wanted for murder. He found many fellow countrymen in Little Italy, including Giuseppe Piddu Morello, whose sister he married, thus tying himself to the Morello-Terranova clan. Ignazio the Wolf, as he came to be called, became one of the leaders of the Black Hand, responsible for at least sixty murders, but when he was finally arrested in 1910 it was for counterfeiting. Released on parole in 1920 he was again imprisoned in July 1936. His name was tied to that of other famous figures, such as Joe Petrosino and Vito Cascio Ferro. He died of natural causes on January 13, 1947, and was buried in the family tomb of the Terranova family in Brooklyn.

Il linguaggio dei cenni della „Mano Nera".

„La polizia ti conosce." „Tu devi cambiare il tuo piano." „Vorrei dirti qualche cosa." „Sii cauto!"

„Va pure!" „Preparati a soccorrermi." „Sta attento!" „Aiutami!"

La polizia degli Stati Uniti è riuscita a fare finalmente un po' di luce in quel buio che fin qui aveva avvolto la misteriosa setta della „Mano Nera". Da poco sono venuti a conoscenza dei funzionari di polizia, i cenni convenzionali ed il modo di spiegare tutti i segni di riconoscimento e di avvertenza, di questa associazione di delinquenti, e così anche noi abbiamo ora l'occasione di fornire ai nostri lettori interessanti particolari in proposito.

Stretta di mano degli affigliati alla „Mano Nera".

Già la stretta di mano che gli affigliati alla „Mano Nera" si scambiano per assicurarsi vicendevolmente che essi fanno parte della setta, ha un significato caratteristico; come pure i segni di avvertimento, che per la loro semplicità non lasciano più nulla a desiderare, offrono a ciascun affigliato, la possibilità di comprendere ed di conoscere, senza errori e senza inganno, tutto ció che deve essergli comunicato.

10. This illustration, part of a collection dedicated to the exploits of Joe Petrosino published in serial form in 1935, shows some conventional gestures used by the criminals of the Black Hand. According to some, the origins of the Black Hand date to the kingdom of Naples during the second half of the eighteenth century. Beginning in 1880 small groups of Italian immigrants, rather than integrate in America, formed criminal gangs that practiced extortion. Their modus operandi was simple and unvarying: the victim was sent a letter threatening kidnapping, financial problems, or even death if a certain sum was not delivered to a certain place; at the bottom of the letter appeared the imprint of a hand accompanied by the image of a skull. Even the celebrated Caruso fell victim to an extortion scheme and decided to pay following the first threat. When the threat was repeated he turned to the police, who arrested the guilty parties. The Black Hand reached the height of its criminal success early in the twentieth century but had disappeared by around 1920.

11. The story of Joe Petrosino (1860–1909) is one of those fatally destined to become legendary. Born in the Campagna region of Italy, he arrived in New York City with his family in 1873, and even as a boy he distinguished himself for industriousness. While studying English, he did not disdain dirtying his hands with humble labors such as shining shoes and sweeping streets. He joined the police force in 1883, and his early years were not easy as the only Italian policeman amid many Jewish and Irish colleagues. But the police needed a man who spoke the new language of criminality, that of the Black Hand and the first Mafia gangs. In 1895 one of the leaders of the police force, the future president of the United States Theodore Roosevelt, promoted him to sergeant and entrusted him with the roll of investigator, saving him from street patrol.

12. The cover of a biographical novel about Joe Petrosino, published in 1935, pictures the Italian-American policeman as more popular than ever twenty-five years after he was assassinated, on the evening of March 12, 1909, struck down by four bullets in Piazza Marina, Palermo. He had arrived in Italy on February 21, intending to collect information on the criminal ties between Sicily and New York. His trip was supposed to be secret, but Theodore A. Bingham, the New York City police commissioner, had incautiously released the information, which reached Don Vito Cascio Ferro in Italy. Bingham was removed from office, while 250,000 New Yorkers accompanied Petrosino's corpse on its last journey. The city had never seen such large-scale attendance of a funeral.

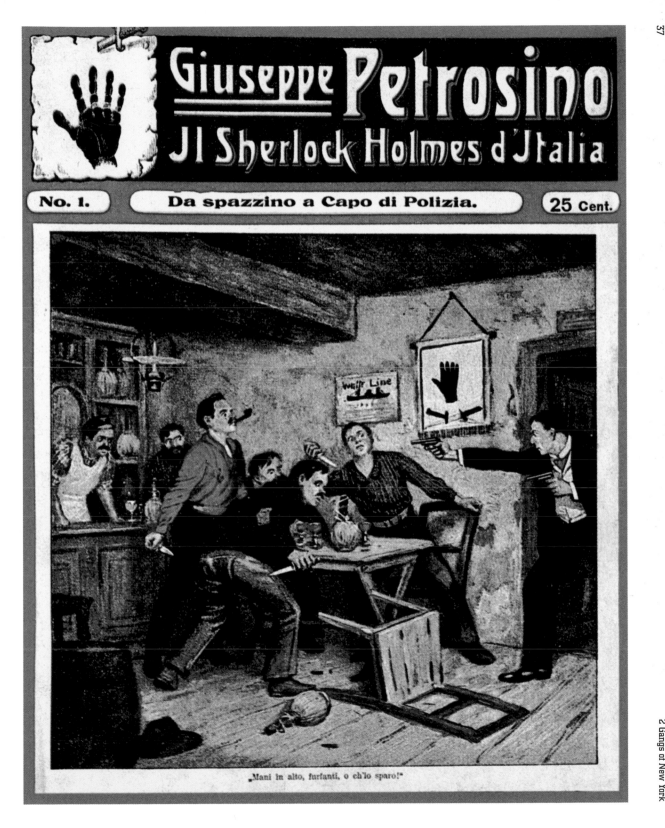

"Mani in alto, furfanti, o ch'io sparo!"

13. Petrosino's career saw one success after another. One case among many—the famous Barrel Murder case—earned him justified fame. Benedetto Madonia had the bad idea of going into competition with Don Vito Cascio Ferro in the territory he controlled and ended up dead, his body stuffed into a barrel. By means of careful investigative work, Petrosino identified those responsible for the murder, forcing Cascio Ferro to make a sudden flight. In 1905, having demonstrated the importance of utilizing police who understood the criminals they were chasing, Petrosino was promoted to lieutenant and was given a unit composed of five Italian policemen and an Irishman who spoke and understood Italian. This unit, called the Italian squad, is portrayed here in a rare period photo.

14. This image, from 1903, shows detective Joe Petrosino (far left) with his colleagues Carey and McCafferty, escorting Thomas Petto (second from left) to prison. Petto, nicknamed the "Ox," was twenty-four and a member of the Morello gang. A pawn ticket found in his pocket tied him to the murder of Benedetto Madonia. Petrosino caught him a few days after the discovery of the body and suspected that Petto was the material author of the murder. The so-called Barrel Murder, however, did not have a happy outcome at trial: between sudden memory losses of witnesses, silences, and retractions, none of the criminals involved was convicted.

3 United Italy Discovers the Mafia

From the Notarbartolo Affair to Benito Mussolini

He was born in Palermo on February 23, 1834, and he tied his noble title of marchese of San Giovanni to battlefield experience as one of Garibaldi's Thousand in the battle at Milazzo, Sicily. But that is not why he has a place in history; rather, Emanuele Notarbartolo holds a record that he would most certainly have chosen to have done without, that of being the first famous victim, the first "excellent cadaver," in the struggle against the Mafia.

He was condemned by his intellectual honesty and by the scrupulous rigor with which he exercised his public role as mayor of Palermo and then as president of the Bank of Sicily. There was then the fatal encounter with the honorable Raffaele Palizzolo who, aside from serving as counselor for the commune of Palermo and being a deputy of the national parliament, trafficked with mafiosi.

It was Palizzolo's habit to meet every morning with a series of petitioners; he received them in his home, the Villarosa Palace, and with every favor he made a bond, an alliance that might prove useful in the future. But the honorable Palizzolo also had business with the Bank of Sicily, loose and often fraudulent operations that Notarbartolo's thoroughness risked bringing to light.

Thus Palizzolo decided that on February 1, 1893, the marchese of San Giovanni must stop being a nuisance and had him stabbed to death on a train traveling between the stations of Termini Imerese and Trabia.

The resulting trial awakened enormous interest, but in the end it resolved nothing, and Palizzolo was able to return to business in 1905. By then, however, he had lost power and influence; his decision to commit murder had attracted too much attention and embarrassed too many associates.

Meanwhile, other criminal figures had come to the fore in Sicily, chief among them Vito Cascio Ferro. Don Vito was an ambiguous figure, first a revolutionary tied to the Sicilian Leagues, then an unquestioned boss and, in the eyes of many, the first true godfather.

During the period of the Notarbartolo trial Cascio Ferro was about forty years old and wasn't even in Italy. In 1901 he had arrived in New York and joined the Morello family and became one of the leading figures in the rackets of the Black Hand. Indeed, there are those who believe it was Cascio Ferro himself who invented the classic extortion formula, "*Fateci vagnari 'u pizzu*" ("Let us wet our beak"), in which *pizzu* means both the beak of a bird and protection money.

Don Vito did not stay long in the United States. Implicated in Joe Petrosino's investigation of the Barrel Murder, he returned to Sicily, but he did not forget the man who had interfered with his plans, and indeed a great many historians are convinced that it was he who ordered the murder of the detective, which took place on the evening of March 12, 1909, in Palermo.

Cascio Ferro's influence on Mafia affairs in America did not end with his flight. It is difficult to determine whether Don Vito planned to export the entire Sicilian organization to New York, but in any case he chose his ambassador from among the criminal entrepreneurs of Castellammare del Golfo. So it was that Salvatore Maranzano arrived in New York in 1925 and immediately presented himself to the Brooklyn boss Cola Schiro.

Unfortunately for Cascio Ferro, his career was soon interrupted when he was arrested by the prefect Cesare Mori, a man even more energetic and determined than he was. The figure of Mori opens the chapter on the controversial relationship between the Mafia and fascism, for years interpreted as a clash without compromise and with exceptional results.

Cesare Mori, a man of proven investigative energy, had gone into early retirement but was called back into service by Mussolini in 1925. Mussolini gave him full powers, and Mori used them in operations of great popular impact. But aside from the arrest of Cascio Ferro and the intuition that a period of isolation in prison would result in the end of his rule, he caught only small fish in his net. The bandits of the village of Gangi, for example, may well have been criminals but they navigated along routes far from those on which the Mafia power sailed.

Instead, fishing around in the turbid waters of the collusions between the Mafia and politicians, Mori uncovered embarrassing and awkward relationships, and when his investigations led him to Alfredo Cucco, the most conspicuous member of the National Fascist Party in Sicily, the decision was made in Rome that it would be better to promote the prefect and appoint him to a more innocuous post among the benches of the Senate.

The outcome of the story merits reflection: first of all, having said good-bye to Cesare Mori, the Mafia bosses involved in his investigations ended up being acquitted or sentenced to such short terms that they soon returned to their traffic; even Alfredo Cucco returned to the ranks and in 1938 was among the signers of Mussolini's Manifesto of Race.

There is, then, the well-founded suspicion that Mussolini, not having available forces to replace the Mafia in the government of the territory, rather than defeat it decided to "regulate" it, allying the bosses to him. Of course in doing so he would have had the support of the Cosa Nostra, which has never shown any qualms about supporting the government in power, at least to all appearances.

An emblematic case is that of Calogero Vizzini, boss of Villalba. Sent into confinement at the border at Chianciano, Don Calò did not stop directing his business, tied most of all to the theft and sale of livestock; he returned home in 1937 and after the Allied landings in Sicily he was even elected mayor of his town.

Another typical figure in the relationship between the Mafia and fascism was Vito Genovese. Acting boss for Lucky Luciano, Genovese was forced to leave New York in 1937, sought for the murder of Ferdinand Boccia, a gambling racketeer who had imprudently tried to claim his share in the profits from a scam.

In Italy Vito Genovese immediately became a major supporter of fascism, but in the immediate postwar period the same Genovese, one of the most evasive and double-dealing bosses in history, found it quite natural to change flags, offering his skills and knowledge to the Allies.

LA LEGGE È EGUALE PER

1. The trial for the murder of Emanuele Notarbartolo, the first "excellent cadaver" in the history of the Mafia, took place in 1901 in the court of Milan. Of noble origins, Notarbartolo founded and directed the Corriere Siciliano in 1869 and later assumed the position of president of Palermo Hospital. From 1873 to 1876 he served as mayor of the city, then became general director of the Bank of Sicily, which he vigorously directed until 1890. After a short period of retirement, Notarbartolo returned to the political and financial scene, discovering serious illicit acts involving the bank and the honorable Raffaele Palizzolo; Notarbartolo threatened to publicly reveal the affairs and collusions. On February 1, 1893, while traveling by train between Termini Imerese and Trabia, he was stabbed to death by Matteo Filippello and Giuseppe Fontana. Raffaele Palizzolo was found guilty of being the instigator of the murder during the first trial, only to be acquitted during the appeals process.

2. Vito Cascio Ferro (1862–1943) is portrayed here around 1920 together with a grandson and hunting dog. First as a young anarchist and then as president of the Sicilian Leagues of Bisacquino, finally mafioso, for many Cascio Ferro was the first true godfather of the Cosa Nostra. Forced to flee during the repression under Crispi, he took shelter first in Tunisia and then, in 1901, in the United States. There he distinguished himself among the leaders of the Black Hand, whose associates threatened their victims with the phrase *Fateci vagnari 'u pizzu*. The investigation into the Barrel Murder case forced him to leave New York for New Orleans, then to return to Sicily, where he exercised absolute power for many years. It was the prefect Mori who put an end to his career. He was arrested in 1927 for the murder of Gioacchino Lo Voi, which had happened four years earlier, and, unlike the many other charges that had come to nothing, this time he was sentenced to life imprisonment. Don Vito died in the prison of Pozzuoli during the American bombardments of 1943: the structure was evacuated and the prisoners transferred elsewhere, but he was forgotten in a cell where, old and ill, he died of thirst.

3. Benito Mussolini posed in 1925 beside a bust of himself, the work of the Swiss sculptor Ernst Dürig. In May of 1924, two years after the fascist March on Rome and just one month before the murder of Giacomo Matteotti, Mussolini traveled to Sicily to get a sense of the island's social and political conditions. During the trip he had an unpleasant experience involving a small-town mayor named Francesco Cuccia who expressed surprise at the size of Mussolini's escort, telling him he had no need of the guards since he was under the protection of the mayor and the mayor's friends. They would guarantee his safety. The ingenuous mayor was unaware of the offense he had caused Mussolini who, back in Rome, gave orders to immediately solve the problem of the Mafia. In truth, many scholars doubt the veracity of this story, but they don't doubt Mussolini's initial determination, which gave full powers to Cesare Mori.

1. CESARE MORI

CESARE MORI

CON LA MAFIA
AI FERRI CORTI

CON 35 ILLUSTRAZIONI
FUORI TESTO

A. MONDADÓRI · EDITORE

4. The story of Cesare Mori (1871–1942) is one of tenacity and ferocious determination. Abandoned by his parents, he grew up in an orphanage in Pavia and as a youth entered the military academy before joining the police. He was given his first post in 1904 in Castelvetrano and he distinguished himself for rough efficiency. Later commissions took him to Florence, Rome, Turin, and Bologna. As police chief in Bologna in 1922, he did not show much respect for the turbulence of the young fascists, treating them as ordinary ruffians; this earned him a bad reputation and he was suspended from service. But in 1925 he was recalled and sent to Sicily, with the task of fighting every form of organized criminality on the island.

5. Cesare Mori was active in Sicily on a mandate from Mussolini from November 1925 until 1929. The methods he employed in opposing the Mafia and banditry were at the limits of legality, and on occasion he went well over those limits, earning him the title "Iron Prefect." His most famous operation was the siege of the village of Gangi, isolated high on a hill at an altitude of more than 3,000 feet. To drive out the criminals who had barricaded themselves in the village Mori brought in a veritable army of policemen and *carabineri*, combing the village house by house. They killed the livestock, capturing women and children to hold as ransom for those who did not surrender.

6. The trials followed the example of firmness set by Cesare Mori, sentencing an impressive number of the accused to prison terms. One such group is portrayed in this photo, taken in Palermo on February 23, 1928. The prefect's investigations uncovered examples of connivance between the Mafia and politicians, even including Alfredo Cucco, one of the most important members of the fascist hierarchy in Sicily. Cucco was expelled from the party in 1927 and put on trial four years later, although the elements necessary to reach a final conviction never surfaced. As the months passed, the Iron Prefect began to pose problems for those who had entrusted him with full powers to fight crime and corruption. The only possible solution was to promote the industrious official, who found himself elevated to the rank of senator.

Mori entrusted the memory of his undertakings in a book, *Con la mafia ai ferri corti* ("At close quarters with the Mafia"), published in the Le Scie series by Mondadori in 1932. He died in Udine ten years later, forgotten by an Italy struggling with the harsh realities of the Second World War.

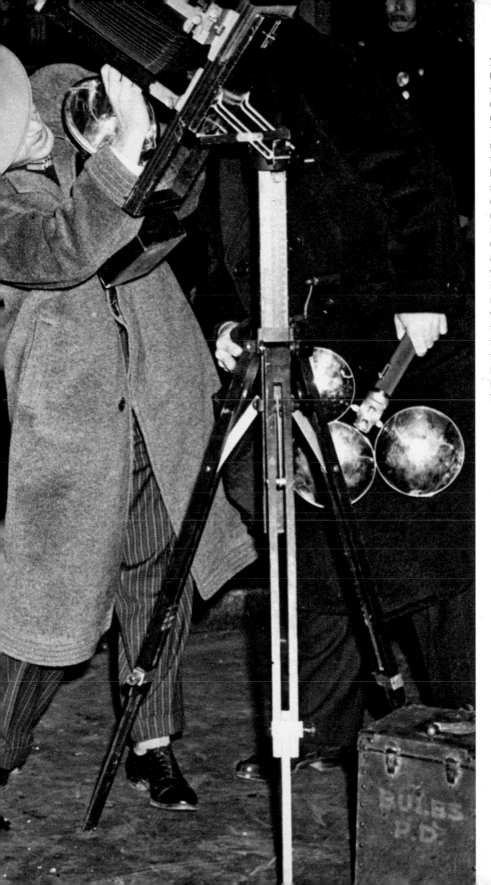

7. January 11, 1943. A New York City police photographer prepares to capture the scene of the murder of Carlo Tresca, killed on the corner of Fifth Avenue and 15th Street. Tresca (1879–1943), an Italian trade unionist forced early on to flee to the United States to avoid prison for his political activities, proved himself over the years a fierce enemy of fascism, using every means to oppose Mussolini's support among immigrant groups. The Cosa Nostra decided to intervene in the unpleasant situation, according to some, with the intention of ingratiating itself with Mussolini. But the crime met with indifference, obscured by worries about the war, which for the Italians was taking a turn for the worse. At the time, investigators were of the opinion that the killing had been carried out by Carmine Galante on the order of Vito Genovese.

Senseless Prohibition

The Golden Age of Mafia Gangsters

From the gangs of New York to the Black Hand to the most notorious gangsters of history the evolution was gradual but steady. Indeed, many future bosses took their first steps as members of criminal gangs active between the end of the nineteenth century and the opening decades of the twentieth.

There was, however, one very important turning point, a moment that can be precisely identified, and it falls on January 16, 1919, the day on which the Eighteenth Amendment to the U.S. Constitution, enabled by the Volstead Act of October 28, 1919, went into effect. Thus it was the day the Prohibition era officially began.

Without doubt, Senator Andrew Volstead was animated by the very best intentions, and these were clearly expressed by the popular Reverend Billy Sunday: "The reign of tears is over. The slums will soon be only a memory. We will turn our prisons into factories and our jails into storehouses and corncribs. Men will walk upright now, women will smile, and the children will laugh. Hell will be forever for rent!"

During the years in which the amendment remained in force, meaning until its repeal in February 1933, it seemed instead that the doors to hell had been swung wide, releasing crimes and violence, prostitution and blackmail, drugs and the corpses of murder victims. By no means, however, was the senator alone in his crusade against alcohol; with him were religious groups and fundamentalist movements that promoted the value of temperance. Associations such as the Anti-Saloon League, the American Temperance Society, and the New York Society for the Suppression of Vice attracted widespread support in the battle for the moralization of America. This was no small thing, since such support meant votes, and votes are always of great interest to politicians, who quickly understood the importance of supporting temperance groups.

The battle involved opium as well as alcohol and extended to sexual practices and risqué publications. Even so, beer and whiskey were the primary targets because historically they represented the most economical means by which the lower levels of society and society's outcasts could forget their worries and miseries, even if only for a few hours. And the relationship between alcohol and loss of control and inhibition and between that loss and crime has been recognized since time immemorial.

As if that weren't enough, there was the awareness that a drunk accomplishes less work, which drew the Rockefellers and the Fords into the fray, saying it was time to stop permitting this and giving their economic as well as political support to the temperance leagues.

Volstead had powerful allies and was certainly speaking from good faith when he affirmed that a new era was about to begin in the United States, but cracks appeared in his utopian vision almost immediately after the stroke of midnight on January 16: a half hour after the law took effect a group of Chicago criminals attacked a train loaded with cases of whiskey and carted off bottles and kegs with a value of $100,000.

A few months passed before the second worrisome sign. Prior to Prohibition, there had been about 15,000 bars in New York City; by the end of 1920 the city had twice that number of speakeasies, clandestine locales one entered by knocking on a certain door and speaking a certain password. Volstead had not calculated that Americans had no intention of giving up drinking, which meant contraband from Mexico and Canada, where the market for alcohol remained open, then clandestine distilleries and money, a great deal of money without taxes and controls.

Some denizens of the underworld seized the opportunity at once, while others were reticent about abandoning the businesses of racketeering and gambling to get into new adventures. One such was the Chicago crime boss Giacomo "Big Jim" Colosimo, and his friends and those who depended on him wasted little time in getting rid of him. The problem was that great profits, far from leading to satiety, result instead in increased greed, and by around 1928 the ranks of the Mafia had been divided into two opposing camps. To one side there was Salvatore Maranzano along with Joe Bonanno, Stefano Magaddino, Joe Profaci, and Joe Aiello, while the other group was led by Joe "the Boss" Masseria and with him Albert Anastasia, Vito Genovese, Frank Costello, Joe Adonis, and Lucky Luciano.

The power struggle soon became war, the so-called Castellammarese War, named for Sicily's Castellammare del Golfo, the birthplace of many of the gangsters involved. The winner, in 1931, was Salvatore Maranzano, in no small part because many of Masseria's allies had betrayed him, changing sides. Having eliminated Masseria, Maranzano reorganized the criminal factions, dividing them into families, and then proclaimed himself *Capo dei capi* ("Boss of the bosses"), a clumsy move that only made him unpopular and eventually drove his associates to kill him.

Maranzano's successor was the man who more than any other contributed to the growth of the Cosa Nostra in the United States, and that man was Salvatore Lucania, far better known as Lucky Luciano.

Luciano did not assume a dictatorial attitude, preferring to keep a low profile, but he sensed the need to establish rules in the world of organized crime so as to avoid a repetition of bloody conflicts, which aside from their cost in human lives and lost business attracted unwanted attention from the police and judges. For this reason he created the Commission, which in its original formula was composed of the bosses of seven families, the five from New York, represented by Luciano, Bonanno, Profaci, Mangano, and Gagliano, to which were added Capone's Chicago Outfit and the Buffalo family of Stefano Magaddino.

The Commission had no boss, at least not of the type understood by Maranzano, and had instead a leader. Luciano performed the role of leader from 1931 to 1936, while in the later period, until 1951, the Commission was governed by an alliance of families.

Although unable to eliminate every dispute or disagreement, the Commission proved an effective structure, directed over the years by such charismatic figures as Carlo Gambino and Vincent Gigante.

1. This illegal storehouse of alcohol was discovered by the New York City police in an attic in Queens Village, Long Island. Visible in the photograph, taken on January 23, 1930, are barrels and distillation vats, each one with a capacity of 25 gallons. Three more years were yet to go before Prohibition ended with the Twenty-first Amendment, which repealed the Volstead Act. In 1930 the power and influence of organized crime were at their highest levels, and in the city of Chicago Al Capone was considered "public enemy number one."

2. Jacksonville, Florida, March 22, 1921. A federal agent demonstrates the contraption used by a smuggler for transporting small quantities of alcohol, which can be served to clients by means of a tap at the bottom of the container.

Prohibition found its paladin in Andrew John Volstead (1860–1947), from Kenyon, Minnesota, who at age forty-three was elected to the U.S. Congress for the Republican Party. He was known for the law he promoted that passed into history as the Volstead Act. Ratified in October 1919 it came into effect the next January and made provisions for enforcement of the Eighteenth Amendment banning the manufacture, transportation, and sale of all types of alcoholic beverages. With this measure the period of Prohibition began, guaranteeing immense fortunes to organized crime.

4. The conflict that broke out in 1929 came to be known as the Castellammarese war, after Castellammare del Golfo, a town in Sicily under the control of Don Vito Cascio Ferro, who sent his most trusted men to New York to take control of criminal activities. Salvatore Maranzano's group, fighting the group under Masseria, included Joe Bonanno, Stefano Magaddino, Joe Profaci, and Joe Aiello. On the opposite side were Al Capone, Lucky Luciano, Albert Anastasia, Vito Genovese, Joe Adonis, and Frank Costello. But before the war ended Lucky and his men had formed a pact with Maranzano. On April 15, 1931, Joe Masseria was seated at a table in his favorite restaurant, the Nuova Villa Tammaro, in Coney Island, playing cards with Luciano. At a certain point Lucky excused himself, saying he had to use the bathroom; this was the signal for the group of hit men composed of Albert Anastasia, Vito Genovese, Bugsy Siegel, and Joe Adonis. Joe the Boss was lying dead on the floor when someone inserted a playing card between his fingers: the ace of spades, bad luck and death in the language of cards.

3. Giuseppe Masseria (1887–1931), known as "Joe the Boss," was born in Sciacca, in the province of Agrigento, and arrived in the United States at the age of sixteen. Initially tied to the Piddu (Giuseppe) Morello gang, he ended up breaking away and later collecting its heredity in the early twenties. Masseria's power extended over the zone of the Lower East Side of Manhattan, while East Harlem and the Bronx were controlled by Ciro Terranova, in partnership with Dutch Schultz. On August 9, 1922, Masseria miraculously escaped an attempt on his life, earning him the epithet "the man who can dodge bullets," something he failed to accomplish nine years later.

5. Salvatore Maranzano (1886–1931) did not long outlive his rival Masseria. Having taken control of New York's organized crime, he proclaimed himself the "Boss of bosses" and convened meetings in which he assumed arrogant attitudes toward the other gangsters. There was also his opposition to Lucky Luciano's contacts with Meyer Lansky and Bugsy Siegel, leading Luciano to plan his elimination. Maranzano tried to make the first move, hiring an Irish hit man named Vincent "Mad Dog" Coll, but he failed to move quickly enough. On September 10, 1931, three men of the Luciano gang showed up at Maranzano's office on the ninth floor of the New York Central Building (today's Helmsley Building) on Park Avenue and stabbed him to death. In coming years most of the men tied to Maranzano moved over to the Bonanno family.

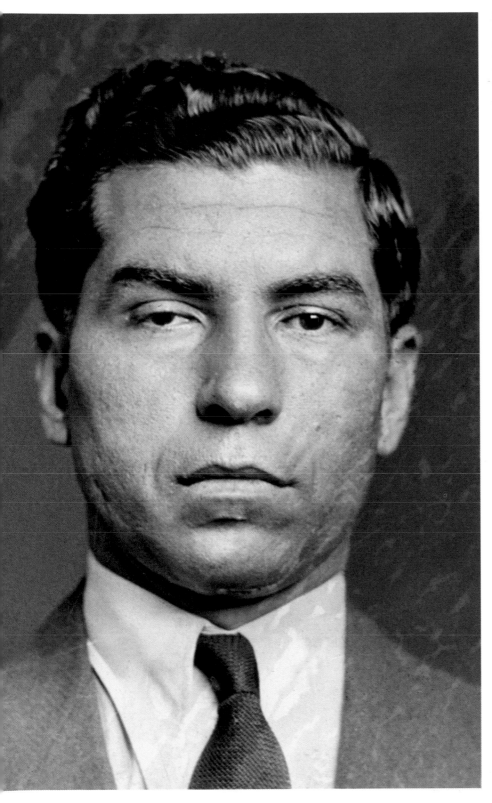

6. The Lucania family was originally from Lercara Friddi, a town in the province of Palermo once famous for its sulfur mines. There were the father, Angelo, mother, Amelia, and five children: Salvatore, the second oldest, born in 1897, was ten when the Lucanias decided to try their luck in America.

His first act on arrival in the United States was to swap the name Salvatore for the more American Charlie; Lucania evolved into Luciano. The second goal to which he dedicated himself was that of surviving the streets of New York. On those streets he encountered boys with names like Meyer Lansky, Bugsy Siegel, and Frank Costello. Together they got involved in thefts and extortion, and as early as 1931 Charlie got his first taste of prison.

He came by the nickname Lucky when he miraculously survived an attack by a rival gang and was left for dead. The turning point came with Prohibition, during which he and his ambitious friends, known collectively as the Young Turks, came into conflict with older members of the Mafia, men who'd arrived in the United States as adults and were known as Mustache Petes because of the fashion among early Italian immigrants to proudly sport oversize mustaches. Two such were Joe Masseria and Salvatore Maranzano.

7. Meyer Lansky in a mugshot taken by the New York City police in 1930. Born in Belarus in 1902 to Polish parents, Majer Suchowljansky arrived in the United States in 1911. His relationship to Bugsy Siegel was of fundamental importance, but even more important was his tie to Lucky Luciano. A curious anecdote is told about their relationship: when both were very young, Luciano took a shot at Lansky, trying to extort small sums of money from him. A violent fistfight put an end to the Italian's bullying behavior and marked the beginning of a close friendship. When Lucky Luciano was arrested Lansky moved his operations to Florida, then New Orleans, and finally to Cuba. Together with Bugsy Siegel he saw the potential of Las Vegas as a gambling capital. In the 1970s, under threat of arrest for tax evasion, Meyer Lansky went to Israel, but he stayed only a short time. He spent the last years of his life isolated in his home in Miami, dying there from lung cancer on January 15, 1983, at the age of eighty.

8. Nicola Sacco (right) was born on April 22, 1891, and Bartolomeo Vanzetti on June 11, 1888. They died together, executed in the electric chair in the penitentiary of Charlestown, Massachusetts, on August 23, 1927. They were accused of having killed a bookkeeper and a guard during the course of the armed robbery of a payroll being delivered to the workers of the Slater and Merrill shoe factory.

The freely given confession of a prisoner, Celestino Madeiros, who admitted to the crime and claimed to have carried it out together with other gangsters of the Butsey Morelli gang was not enough to save Sacco and Vanzetti. In 1973 confirmation that Morelli was responsible for the bloody attack was provided by another gangster, Vincent Teresa. Teresa said Morelli had told him, "Those two grease-

balls took it on the chin. They got in our way so we just ran over them." The story of Sacco and Vanzetti has inspired protests and movements, novels and ballads. In 1977, on the fiftieth anniversary of the execution, Massachusetts governor Michael Dukakis proclaimed August 23 Sacco and Vanzetti Memorial Day and said the two had been the victims of "proceedings . . . permeated with unfairness."

9. Known as the Chicago Outfit, it was the principal Mafia organization active outside New York City in the opening decades of the twentieth century. Its first leader was Giacomo Colosimo (1878–1920), known as "Big Jim," shown here in a photograph with the very young Dale Winter, a singer he married after divorcing his first wife. Colosimo had a passion for women as well as for the opera and food, and he even opened his own restaurant, Colosimo's Café, which boasted the best service and best chef in the city.

Big Jim had arrived in the United States very early, in 1895, and had lost no time in assembling a criminal empire, but his resistance to change and the exaggerated passions that so totally occupied him led Johnny Torrio, a relative of his by marriage and an enforcer Colosimo had brought to Chicago from New York, to see him as an obstacle. Torrio summoned the young Alphonse Capone from New York, and with the help of Frankie Yale, on May 11, 1920, set up a deadly trap for Big Jim.

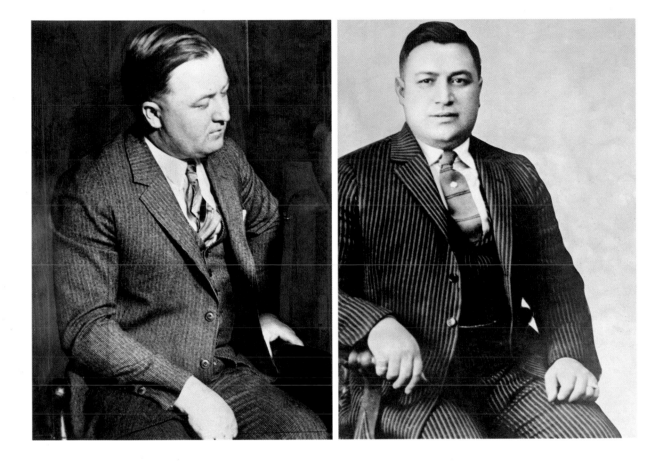

10. Without doubt, the Irish-born Dion O'Banion (1892–1924), shown above, was the primary enemy of Johnny Torrio and Al Capone in the struggle for control of Chicago's criminal enterprises during the early years of Prohibition. O'Banion is thought to have been raking in up to $1 million a year from the trade in illegal alcohol. After an early attempt to reach an agreement to divide up the territory, O'Banion came into conflict with the Chicago Outfit, Torrio's gang, and its allies, the criminal gang of the Genna brothers. The gangster Mike Merlo and the Sicilian Union sought in vain to mediate the clash, and Merlo's death—of natural causes—sped up events. The morning of November 10, 1924, Frankie Yale, together with Torrio's hit men Frank Scalice and Albert Anselmi, burst into O'Banion's flower store and killed their thirty-two-year-old business rival. The murder unleashed a struggle between the North Side gang and the Chicago Outfit that was to last four years, ending in the St. Valentine's Day Massacre of February 14, 1929.

11. Frankie Yale was born Francesco Ioele in Longobucco in the province of Cosenza on January 22, 1893, and arrived in the United States at the age of eight. His first arrest, for vandalism, dated to 1912, but his meeting with Johnny Torrio changed his life, introducing him to the Five Points gang. When Torrio moved to Chicago, in 1915, he left Yale in New York as his trusted representative; and in Brooklyn Yale met the young Capone. During the early twenties Yale's principal enemy was William Lovett, known as "Wild Bill"; Lovett tried to eliminate his rival, who escaped the attack, albeit with serious wounds. The vendetta came two years later when Yale's men, including the gangster Vincent Mangano, killed Lovett.

12. On July 1, 1928, Yale was in his usual Brooklyn hangout, the Sunrise Club, when he received a phone call. His wife, Lucy, was having problems and it would be best if he could hurry home. The call was a trick to lure him into a trap. He set off for home in his car but at the first intersection noted there were four men in the Buick close behind. Yale sped up to get away, but the Buick caught up to him and its occupants fired off a burst. Yale's car skidded out of control and crashed into the front stairs of a house, with his body thrown out of the vehicle. When the police arrived at the scene they found the arrangement immortalized in the photo above. In all likelihood Frankie's killers were men working with his ex-associate Capone. Relations with him had been chilly since the spring of 1927.

13. Frankie Yale's funeral turned into a spectacular event of a kind never before seen in the streets of Brooklyn. Colorful heaps of flowers carpeted the sidewalks, a hundred cars with mourners followed the hearse on which the gangster's silver coffin rested upon a catafalque. The cortege was not without its theatrical moments, such as when a woman burst out of the crowd of onlookers lined up along the streets and rushed at the coffin, spitting at it. She was later found to be the widow of one of the many men whose paths had crossed that of Frankie Yale and who had paid for the encounter with their life.

MENS CELLROOM

14. The date of this photo is November 22, 1927, and the caption that accompanies it needs no comment: "It is reported that gangsters have been imported from New York, St. Louis, and San Francisco in the recent gang war that was revealed in Chicago yesterday. Machine guns were found in the Atlantic Hotel, trained on a cigarstore across the street which is known to be frequented by Al Capone and Antonio Lombardo,

head of the Sicilian Union. Police say the two men were marked for death. Leaders of the opposing faction, Michael Bizzarro, Joseph Aiello (leader of the gang that opposes Capone), Joseph Rubinello, Jack Monzello, and Joseph Russo (from left to right), were rounded up by the police and brought downtown. All have long criminal records, and the police orders are now to kill them on the slightest sign of resistance."

15. Giovanni Torrio (1882–1957) was born in Irsina, a hamlet near Matera, and lost his father at a young age. On his arrival in the United States he became Johnny and soon saw the addition of the nicknames "the Brain" as well as "the Fox." His astuteness enabled him to eliminate enemies, some famous, some less so, beginning with the period he spent with Paul Kelly and the Five Points gang, to pass to Big Jim Colosimo and Dion O'Banion. His cunning was of no aid to him on January 24, 1925, when he fell victim to a trap. He

escaped but spent ten days in a coma, while his friend Capone put all his men around the hospital to keep those who had begun the work from getting the idea of finishing it. Torrio never fully recovered from the wounds suffered and, an exceptional case in the story of organized crime, left his business and retired to Italy, with his wife and mother. He returned to the United States at an advanced age and died of a heart attack at seventy-five while sitting in a barber chair, on April 16, 1957.

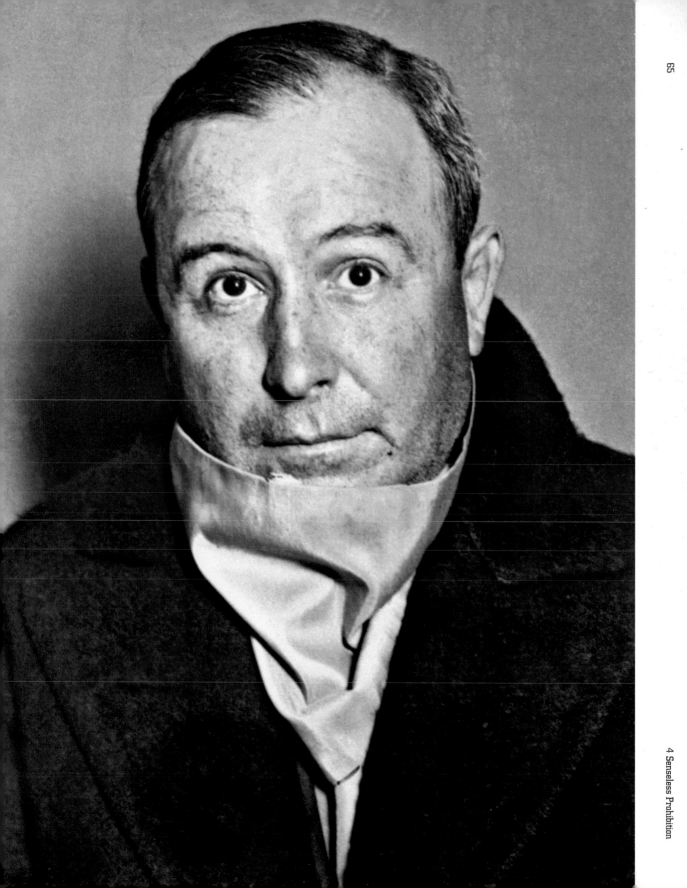

16. J. Edgar Hoover (1895–1972; shown here standing at the center behind the seated President Franklin D. Roosevelt) joined the Bureau of Investigation, which later became the Federal Bureau of Investigation—the FBI—in 1921. He led the FBI from 1935 to 1972, longer than any other director, becoming one of the most powerful and feared men in the United States. The photo above shows FDR signing an act that conferred greater powers on the bureau in its struggle against crime. The relationship between Hoover and the Cosa Nostra is still difficult to understand. Pitiless in his hunt for such outlaws as John Dillinger and Baby Face Nelson, and equally zealous in his treatment of domestic subversives and radical movements, he nevertheless played down the existence of the Mafia, attracting criticism and suspicion.

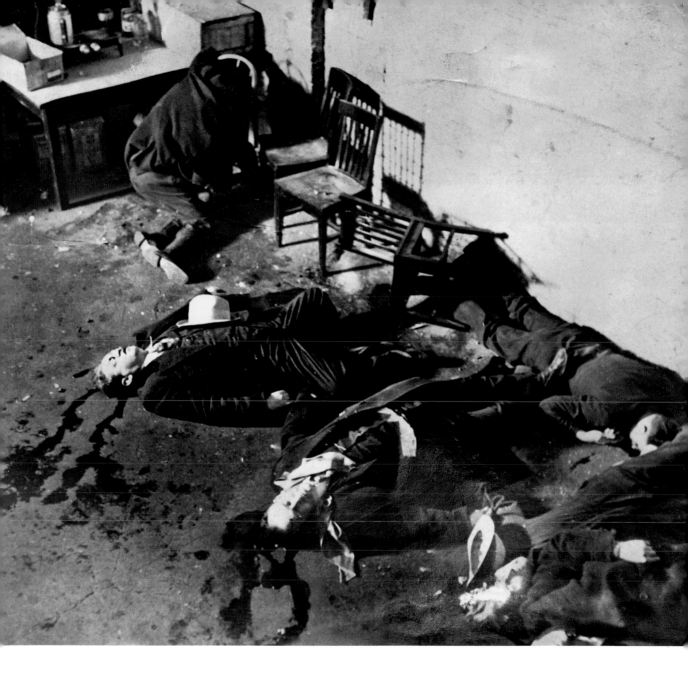

17. February 14, 1929, has entered history as the date of the St. Valentine's Day Massacre. The victims were Peter Gusenberg, Adam Heyer, James Clark, Albert Weinshank, John May, and Reinhart Schwimmer, all members of the North Side gang of Bugs Moran, the successor to Dion O'Banion and a rival of Al Capone in Chicago. Bugs was the target of the attack, but on that day, by chance, he was not with his men. Two of the intruders were dressed as policemen, and having burst into the garage at 2122 North Clark Street they ordered all those present to line up with their faces to the wall. Moran's men at first thought this was a routine check and that it would be over in a few minutes, and by the time they realized it was otherwise it was too late. Other hit men joined the first and opened fire with their .45-caliber Thompson machine guns, the famous tommy guns.

18. To understand the dynamics of the slaughter, or perhaps just to create a nice picture for the photographers, the Chicago police simulated the slaughter, playing the roles of victims and killers. The first man in front of the leveled guns, caught as he observes the men lined up along the wall, is the Cook County coroner Herman N. Bundesen. Despite various investigative hypotheses, many doubts still surround the actual reason for the massacre.

19. Alphonse Gabriel Capone (1899–1947) is shown here seated in the foreground during a picnic together with relatives and friends. Also on hand are several body-guards, easily identifiable by the jackets they wear to hide their holsters and guns. Capone was among the few gangsters of the period who was born in America. His family, originally from Castellammare di Stabia, in the province of Naples, immigrated in 1893 and settled in Brooklyn, where the young Capone distinguished himself early on for aggression and boldness. The first result was a stabbing that disfigured his face and earned him the nickname he himself hated: Scarface. The scar was nothing he could be proud of, resulting as it did from a dispute with a minor hood named Frank Galluccio. Capone had bothered Galluccio's sister, coming on to her in a bar, and for that he earned the quick swipe of a knife and a wound that was poorly sewn up.

20. Al Capone married so young, before being twenty-one, he needed a certificate of consent from his parents. His wife, Mary Couglin, two years older than he was, gave him their single child, Albert Francis, called Sonny. In this photo, taken in 1931, Al and little Sonny attend a charity baseball game between the Chicago White Sox and the Cubs. During a break in the action Gabby Hartnett of the Cubs, destined to be chosen as the best player in the Major League season of 1935, signed a ball for Capone junior.

21. It was September 29, 1930, when Matthew Capone (1908–1967) was taken into custody by Lieutenant Frank Alderhover, who took him to the station in handcuffs. Known to everyone as Mattie or Matt, Matthew was the last of the Capone brothers. Beginning in the middle of the twenties he met and had a good relationship with Mickey Cohen, a gangster who made a name for himself on the West Coast and who later revealed how Matt rankled at having to depend on the more famous Alphonse. During the forties Matt was involved in a murder case, but there was not enough proof to charge him. He died on January 31, 1967, at the age of fifty-nine. So few mourners attended his funeral that a pair of reporters had to set down their notebooks and cameras to help carry the coffin to its final resting place.

22. This photo was taken at Chicago's Detective Bureau, where this man showed up and asked if anyone wanted to speak to him. His name is Rocco Fanelli, body-guard to Al Capone, and along with Jack "Machine Gun" McGurn he has been recognized as having been among those responsible for the massacre of Bugs Moran's men. Despite his appearance, Fanelli was a merciless killer. His poor vision mattered little since his weapon of choice was a submachine gun capable of spitting out hundreds of rounds a minute.

23. Capone is shown here between his lawyers during the grand jury session that charged him with tax evasion. Capone ranks among the most famous gangsters of all time, but his fame is unjustified. While his mentor Johnny "the Brain" Torrio directed the business and kept himself in the shadows, Capone loved the limelight, photos, newspaper headlines, memorable statements; he was brazen enough to offer suggestions to the president of the United States on how to overcome the economic crisis of 1929. When he arrived at Alcatraz after his 1932 arrest, his fellow prisoners kicked him and jeered him with a play on his name (capon), calling him the "castrated cock." Syphilis in the last stage struck his brain, and his capabilities declined so rapidly that the authorities were induced to grant him parole in 1939. He died of a heart attack on January 25, 1947, by which time he had lost his mental facilities completely despite his young age. In fact he was only forty-eight.

24. Eliot Ness (1903–1957) is the most famous agent in the history of the U.S. Treasury Department. It was in part thanks to his unit, the famous Untouchables, that it was possible to stop Al Capone, charging him not so much for the dozens of murders committed but rather for income tax evasion. After this success, Ness was promoted director of public safety in Cleveland, but his career suffered a hard blow with the unsolved crime of the serial killer known as the "Mad Butcher," who killed thirteen times between 1935 and 1938, although some hold he may have had more than forty victims, all in the area between Cleveland, Pittsburgh, and Youngstown. With a few exceptions the identity of these victims has never been established.

25. George Clarence Moran, best known as "Bugs" (on the left in the photo opposite), was born in St. Paul, Minnesota, on August 21, 1891, and had Polish and Irish blood in his veins. He arrived in Chicago in 1910, at the age of nineteen, and had been jailed three times before he turned twenty. Inheriting O'Banion's position, he first battled Johnny Torrio, then Al Capone. With the end of Prohibition he moved to Ohio, where he dedicated himself to bank heists with pitiful results compared to the golden age of American gangsterism. Arrested in 1946 and sentenced to ten years, he had just been freed when he was arrested again, for an old crime for which he had not yet served time. He died of cancer in the penitentiary of Leavenworth in 1957, at the age of sixty-five.

26. They were called the "Terrible Gennas," the six Sicilian brothers who divvied up the territory of Chicago during the twenties. Angelo was the cruelest, coming to be called "Bloody Angelo." After the departure of Torrio and the death of O'Banion the Gennas found themselves fighting the men of Bugs Moran. On May 25, 1925, Angelo fell in an ambush, probably from shots fired by Vincent Drucci and Earl Weiss, hit men tied to Moran. But others say it was Capone who ordered the hit with the purpose of taking over part of the Gennas' business while carrying on his war against Bugs Moran. The large funeral cortege for Angelo's last journey moved through the crowded streets of Chicago to the family chapel in the Mount Carmel cemetery.

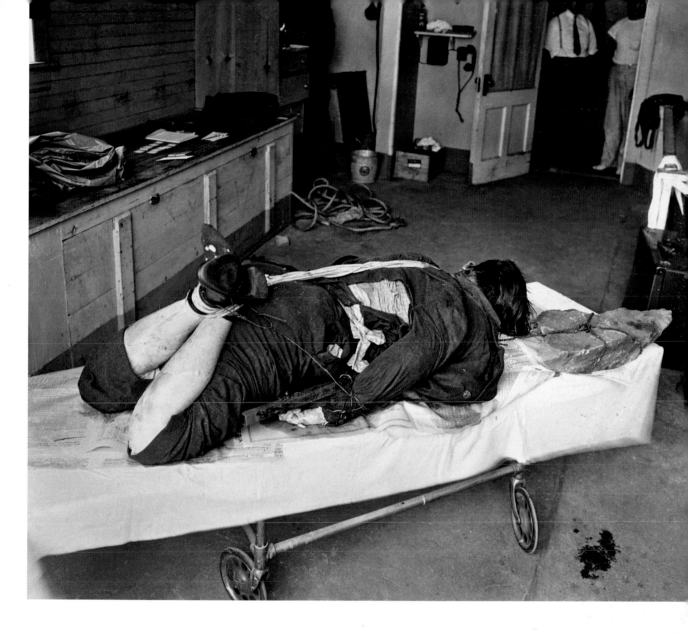

27. The body in the car, struck by numerous bullets, is that of Edward Joseph O'Hare (1893–1939), at the time director of a thriving law office in Cicero, Illinois. He met Capone and became his lawyer, but when Scarface came into the sights of the Treasury Department O'Hare agreed to collaborate with the government, resulting in a key text in the conviction of the gangster.

When the lawyer left his office on that afternoon of November 8, 1939, he took with him a semiauto-matic, which was not at all one of his habits. While driving his Lincoln Zephyr coupe he was flanked by a dark-colored sedan with two killers who opened fire. The execution took place one week before Capone's release from Alcatraz for health reasons. O'Hare's son Edward Henry "Butch," a Second World War naval aviator and winner of the Medal of Honor, brought honor to the family name, and Chicago's international airport is today named for him.

28. Walter Sage was a hit man in the service of the New York boss Abe Reles. Or at least he was until it was revealed he had been skimming off part of the profits from slot machines in Sullivan County. He was then tied up *incaprettamento* style and thrown into Swan Lake attached to a rock. *Incaprettamento*, so called for its resemblance to the way young goats are tied for slaughter, involves tying the victim's hands and feet behind his back then passing the rope around his neck. The knees are bent at 90 degrees so that it is the victim himself, through muscular weariness, who gradually lowers his legs, strangling himself. A warning in the form of a body, a bit of advice impossible to ignore.

29. Francesco Raffaele Nitto (1881–1943), known as Frank Nitti and also as the "Enforcer," was eighteen years older than Capone and together with him was sent to prison for tax evasion. Capone was sentenced to eleven years but Nitti got away with just eighteen months, and as soon as he was released he took command of the Chicago Outfit, with the approval of its boss. Frank behaved well during his time in prison, but he had a problem hardly suitable for a criminal; he suffered claustrophobia and, as soon as the iron bars closed, he was gripped by terrible fits of anxiety, so bad he had to be moved to the infirmary. Under his guidance the Outfit extended its business, tied to prostitution and gambling, expanding it to the control of unions and extortion. In 1939, after the murder of the lawyer O'Hare, Frank Nitti married the lawyer's former girlfriend Ursula Sue Granata.

30. In 1943 Hollywood's major film studios—Columbia, Metro Goldwyn Mayer, Paramount, and Twentieth Century–Fox—reported to the authorities an attempt by the Chicago Outfit to extort $2 million. An FBI informant heard Frank Nitti referred to as the planner of the shakedown, and the Enforcer once again found himself running the risk of ending up in prison, an unacceptable notion for the claustrophobic gangster. On March 19, Nitti drank himself senseless then left home, taking along a .32-caliber revolver, with which he shot himself in the head. He was scheduled to appear before the grand jury the very next day.

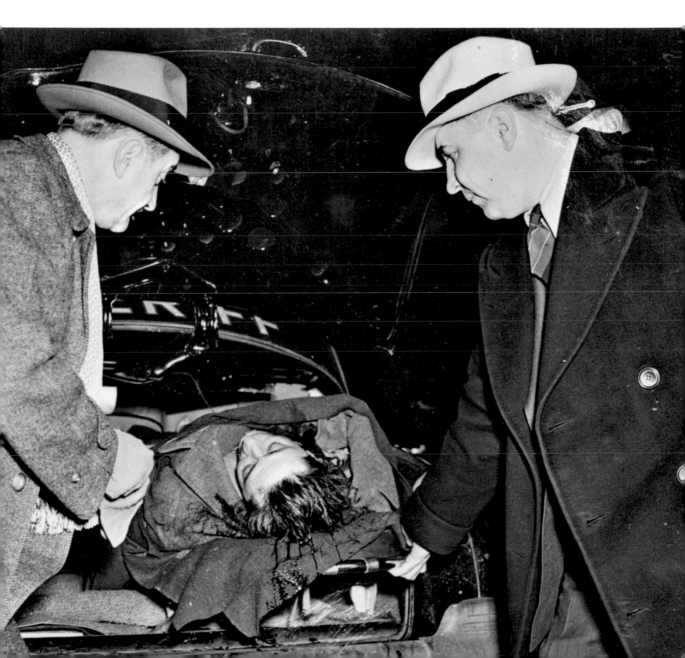

31. From left to right, their names are Harry Straus, Harry Malone, and Frank Abbondando. The photograph portrays them in a police station in New York City, on March 7, 1940, arrested along with nine other criminals. The district attorney William O'Dwyer charged them with responsibility for twelve murders and involvement in another twenty-one. They were part of an organized group known as Murder Inc., a term coined by a journalist to describe their gangland industry. During the thirties and forties hundreds of victims fell to the bullets of this group's hit men, carrying out orders received from the various Mafia families. Among the promoters of Murder Inc. were Albert Anastasia, Lepke Buchalter, and Joe Adonis, with Frankie Carbo ranked among the most popular killers.

32–33. Dutch Schultz's real name was Arthur Simon Flegenheimer (1902–1935); he was born in Manhattan and of Jewish origins, like Meyer Lansky and Bugsy Siegel. Dutch's career as a criminal began in the speakeasy run by the gangster Joey Noe, who decided he wanted to have Schultz around. Schultz's ascent was rapid and, in acquiring control of new territory, he came into conflict with Ciro Terranova and then with Salvatore Maranzano. Early in the thirties he was the most powerful criminal in New York and was deemed "public enemy number one" both by the mayor Fiorello LaGuardia and by the prosecutor Thomas E. Dewey. Dutch Schultz survived at least twenty-five attempts on his life as well as repeated attempts to incriminate him, until the Cosa Nostra finally decided he was out of control, too powerful and too unstable.

It was just past ten on the night of October 23, 1935, at the Place Chophouse in Newark, New Jersey, when a group of hit men attacked Schultz and his men. Dutch survived, but only for about thirty hours, before the wounds to his stomach gave him fulminating peritonitis. Before dying he asked for a priest and then let himself go in a long more or less lucid monologue, faithfully written down by a police stenographer, in what remains one of the most bizarre spiritual testaments of a boss of organized crime.

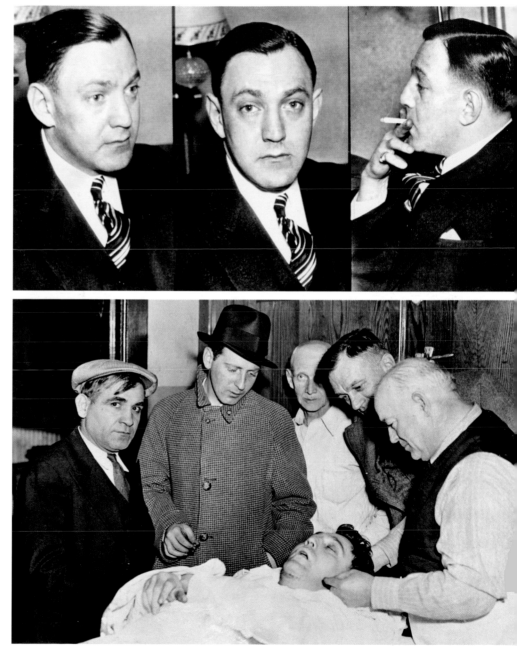

34—35—36. Today it's called Ukraine, but at the end of the 1800s the town of Letychiv still belonged to the territory of Podolia, part of the endless Russian empire. From here arrived the family of Benjamin Siegelbaum, quickly transformed into the simpler Siegel. Benjamin, known as "Bugsy," was born in Brooklyn on February 28, 1906, and as a boy made friends with Meyer Lansky, with whom he shared Jewish roots.

Over the years he met and came into relationships with Lucky Luciano, Frank Costello, Albert Anastasia; together with Anastasia, Vito Genovese, and Joe Adonis he was part of the team of hit men that eliminated Joe Masseria. In 1937 Siegel was sent to California to enlarge the Cosa Nostra's business through an alliance with the local boss Jack Dragna, and in Los Angeles he took on the young Mickey Cohen as a lieutenant.

Siegel's opportunity of a lifetime came during the postwar period when the Mafia decided to transform Las Vegas and the Nevada desert into an endless source of earnings thanks to the legalization of gambling. Siegel was entrusted with the Flamingo Hotel project, which soon proved to be a money pit quite capable of swallowing up vast sums. Siegel complained that estimates were never respected, but both Lansky and Luciano were convinced their associate was skimming the expenses, pocketing money destined for the hotel's construction. They decided to give Siegel a last chance, letting him open the Flamingo to see if the casino would earn back the money invested in it.

Instead, the opening proved a disaster. The invited celebrities found themselves in a hotel still half built with systems that didn't work, including the all-important air-conditioning, which from time to time suddenly shut off. The Flamingo was closed to the public and remained closed until March 1947.

On the evening of June 20, 1947, Siegel was comfortably seated on the sofa in his Beverly Hills home. Busy reading the *Los Angeles Times* he cannot have noticed the man who fired a rifle through the window. The bullets shattered the window, striking the gangster in the head (the following pages show the ticket attached to the big toe of his corpse). No one was ever charged for the murder, which remains officially unsolved.

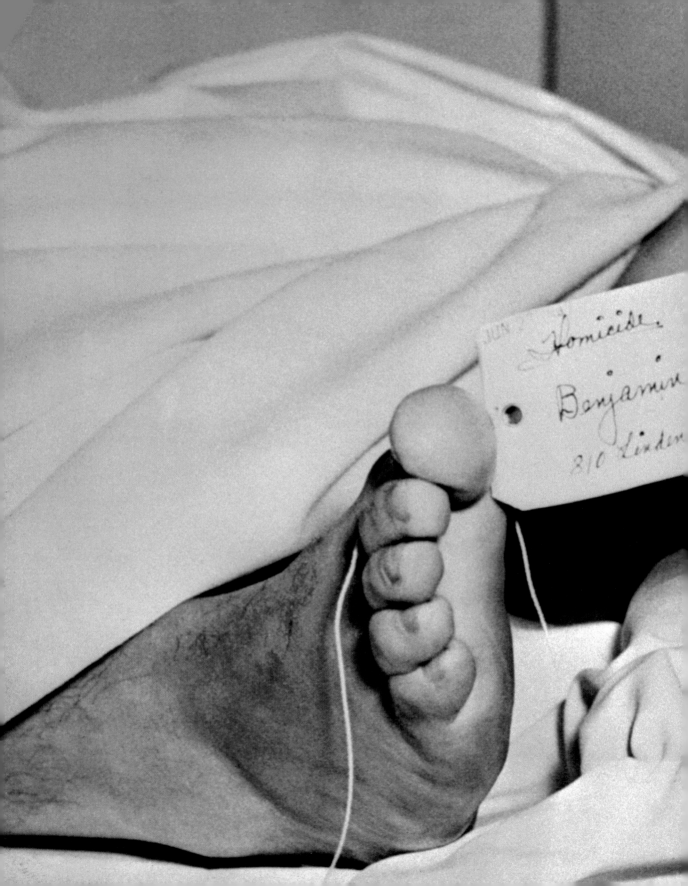

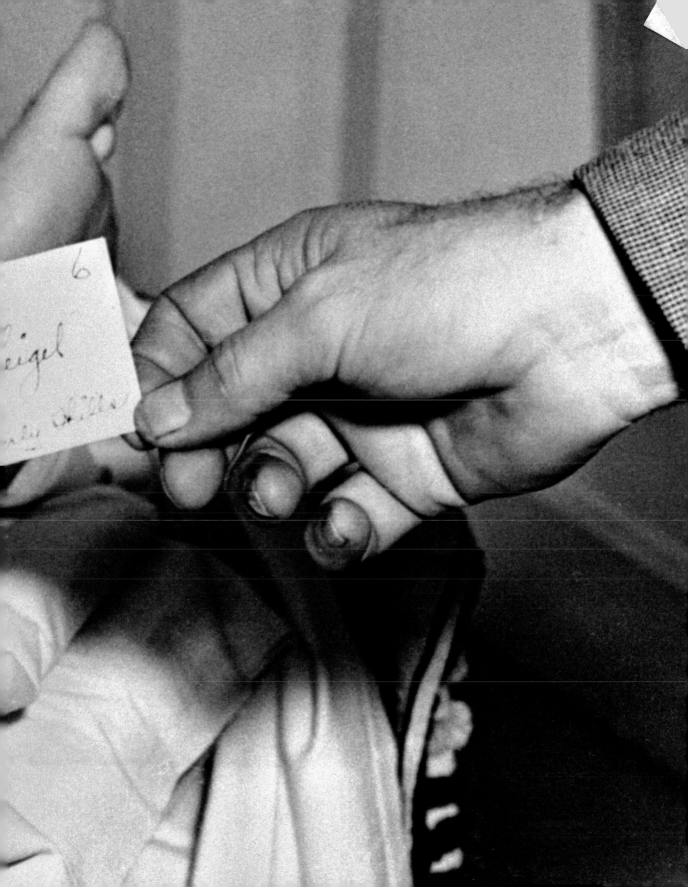

37. Her name was Virginia Hill and she was born in Lipscomb, Alabama, on August 26, 1916. A beautiful girl, at the age of seventeen she began making her living as a prostitute. During the forties she moved to California, where she met Bugsy Siegel and became his lover. He showered her with gifts and dubbed her the "Flamingo," because of her long legs.

Ten days before the gangster was killed, a violent argument between the two drove Hill to abandon him and take off on a European vacation.

This photo, taken March 15, 1951, shows Virginia Hill during a hearing of the Kefauver commission created to investigate organized crime. Questioned about her relationship with the criminal Joe Epstein, Hill responded with a remark that has become historic in part because the hearings were broadcast live by radio throughout the country.

Senator Tobey: "Miss Hill, would you explain to us the source of the money in your possession?"

The witness: "Gifts."

Senator Tobey: "But why would Joe Epstein give you all that money, Miss Hill?"

The witness: "You really want to know?"

Senator Tobey: "Yes, I really want to know."

The witness: "Then I'll tell you why. Because I'm the best cocksucker in town!"

Senator Tobey: "Order! I demand order!"

Of course, the transmission was immediately ended but by then the famous words had been spoken.

38. Achille La Guardia came from Cerignola, Apulia, and was the leader of a musical band when, on tour in Trieste, he met the young Irene Coen Luzzatto and fell hopelessly in love. The happy couple moved to the United States and their son Fiorello Henry La Guardia was born in New York on December 11, 1882.

At around age twenty Fiorello obtained his first postings with the American consulates of Budapest, Trieste, and Fiume, giving him the opportunity to learn several languages so that when he returned to New York he was hired by the U.S. immigration service on Ellis Island.

With a degree in law, in 1915 he became deputy attorney general of New York, and the next year he was the first Italian American elected to the U.S. Congress, with the Republican Party. He served in Congress for five consecutive terms.

From 1934 to 1945 he was mayor of New York City, and despite his sometimes theatrical behavior—as shown above in a 1934 photograph in which he personally smashes confiscated slot machines—he became famous as a tough and incorruptible administrator. His enemies were not limited to the families of the Cosa Nostra and included American Nazi groups; when these referred to him as the Jewish mayor of New York, La Guardia responded, without missing a beat, "My mother undoubtedly had Jewish blood in her veins, but I never thought I had enough in mine to justify boasting about it."

He died of cancer on September 20, 1947. One of New York's airports still bears his name, emblematic of the great affection the people of the city felt for him.

39. Thomas Edmund Dewey (1902–1971) was one of the most popular politicians in the state of New York and also beyond. Gover-nor from 1943 to 1955, he ran for president on the Republican Party ticket in 1944 and again in 1948, losing first to Franklin Roosevelt then Truman. He earned notoriety when he was appointed (1935) special prosecutor to investigate organized crime and was elected district attorney for New York County (1937). Deter-mined to effectively fight organized crime, he assembled a team of sixty-odd collaborators, including assistants and investigators, and Fiorello La Guardia put a like num-ber of policemen at his disposal. His main objective was the incrimina-tion of Dutch Schultz, but he also took on the prostitution business and found proof and witnesses that led to the arrest and conviction of Lucky Luciano. After serving a third term as governor he abandoned pol-itics for private practice. He died of a heart attack at sixty-eight, on March 16, 1971.

40. Louis Buchalter (1897–1944) holds the hardly enviable record of being the only major boss of organized crime to be executed in the United States.

Nicknamed by his mother "Lepke," meaning "little Louis" in Yiddish, in the thirties Buchalter took control of Murder Inc. together with Anastasia, known as the "Mad Hatter." His decline began around 1935. He was found guilty of drug trafficking and was sent to the federal prison at Leavenworth, Kansas. Then, in 1940, he was charged with the murder of a Brooklyn businessman named Joseph Rosen, which had occurred four years earlier.

The photo here, taken on July 20, 1943, in Albany, New York, shows him arriving at court in a car of the penitentiary administration accompanied by an armed guard. From there he was soon to hear the sentence that condemned him to death. On March 4, 1944, an electric charge put an end to his life in the famous penitentiary, Sing Sing, on the banks of the Hudson.

5 An Obscure Period

From the Landings in Sicily to the Giuliano Enigma

It's the night between July 9 and 10, 1943. Seven divisions under the command of the American general George S. Patton and the Briton Bernard Law Montgomery land at three different points on the Sicilian coast. Code-named Operation Husky, the landings meet German and Italian resistance, but fewer than forty days are needed to complete the liberation of the island of Sicily.

Even on this occasion, there are those who speak of an understanding between the secret services and the Mafia, of information and logistics provided to the Allies in exchange for future favors. The truth is that no document exists attesting to any such understanding, although contacts are known to have been made between the two groups following the institution of AMGOT (Allied Military Government of Occupied Territories). In the occupied territories, which were without a legitimately recognized government, AMGOT performed the role of ensuring the functioning of all administrative tasks, from security to labor to matters of health.

After governing Sicily and then all of Italy, the administration performed its role in Germany, Austria, the Low Countries, and Japan, meeting problems, however, in France and Denmark, where it was rapidly replaced by local structures supported by the immediate popular response. In Sicily, AMGOT was directed by Colonel Charles Poletti, who in turn answered to Major General Francis Rodd and above him British general Harold Alexander, and it operated on the island until the end of 1945.

During this period, from 1943 to 1945, many Mafia bosses, out of view during the conflict, returned to the scene and reclaimed the power they had never truly relinquished. They were capable of providing a kind of local government, relieving the Americans of many burdens, for which reason a person like Calogero Vizzini was able to become mayor of Villalba and Giuseppe Genco Russo, with his record wiped clean of dozens of murders, could undertake a political career. While there may be no proof of a relationship between the Cosa Nostra and the Allies before the landings, there are many public documents open to consultation that relate to the later period. For example, a dossier from the OSS, the organization that later became the CIA, reports that the Mafia is capable of reestablishing and guaranteeing social order, adding that the Sicilian bosses can count on the support of more than 90 percent of their fellow citizens.

It should be added that during the first years of the postwar period the United States was worried about the communist threat and saw the Mafia as an ally able to keep the left from taking too much power. In addition to the Mafia there were also the separatist movements and the paramilitary groups supported by the security services.

The figure of Salvatore Giuliano must be seen as inscribed against the background of this scenario; he was a puppet manipulated by "secret" powers and by the Cosa Nostra more than he was a romantic bandit. First he was given arms, then he was goaded on to gestures of dramatic brutality, such as the slaughter of Portella della Ginestra, and in the end he was ejected and eliminated because he was too visible and embarrassing.

Between the end of the forties and the early fifties the criminal scene in Sicily was dominated first by Don Calogero Vizzini and then by his heir Giuseppe Genco Russo, without forgetting that a young *picciotto*, Luciano Liggio, was earning fame in Corleone. He was the one who killed the trade unionist Placido Rizzotto in 1948, on the order of his boss, the doctor Michele Navarra, and Liggio could count on a group of men a few years younger than he was, of whom we will soon speak. Their names were Totò Riina, Bernardo Provenzano, and Calogero Bagarella.

In October 1957, precisely between noon and four o'clock, another turning point in the history of the Mafia took place in rooms of the Grand Hotel des Palmes in Palermo. It is difficult to determine whether this was a summit or rather a series of conversations, but the figures who met and talked in the luxury hotel included the Americans Joe Bonanno, Carmine Galante, and Lucky Luciano, while the representatives of Italy included Giuseppe Genco Russo, Gaetano Badalamenti, Angelo La Barbera, Salvatore Ciaschiteddu (usually translated as "Little Wine Jug") Greco, and Tommaso Buscetta.

One of the subjects taken up concerned the trafficking of drugs, until then of marginal importance in the business interests of the Sicilian Cosa Nostra. Most of the Mafia's earnings came from extortion and control of construction, leaving the European heroin market in the hands of other criminal groups, primarily Corsicans and Marseillais. Joe Bonanno proposed establishment of a new Palermo–New York route along which millions of dollars of drugs could be moved.

There was then another matter to discuss, according to the testimony of Tommaso Buscetta, which took place during dinner; the speaker was again Joe Bananas, as he was known to the Americans. Wouldn't it be a good idea, he suggested, for the Italian Mafia to adopt the model of a commission in the style of the one set up by Lucky Luciano in the United States a few years ago?

The proposal was accepted, and the first Commission had as its leader Salvatore Greco, who directed it from 1957 to 1963. He was flanked by various members, each known for his neighborhood, or mandamento: Calcedonio di Pisa for Noce, Michele Cavataio for Acquasanta, Antonio Matranga for Resuttana, Mariano Troina for San Lorenzo, Angelo and Salvatore La Barbera for Palermo Centro, Cesare Manzella for Cinisi, Antonio Salomone for San Giuseppe Jato, Giuseppe Panno for Casteldaccia, Francesco Sorci for Villagrazia, Lorenzo Motisi for Pagliarelli, Mario Di Girolamo for Corso Calatafimi, and Salvatore Manno for Boccadifalco.

The Commission remained in power until 1963 and the so-called First Mafia War. It was disbanded and then reformed, in 1970, under the guidance of Gaetano Badalamenti.

1. Robert Capa took this photograph on August 4 or 5, 1943. It portrays an elderly Sicilian peasant indicating to an American soldier where the Germans have gone.

Capa (1913–1954) was among the most famous war correspondents, and he accompanied the American troops during the week of battle that led to the conquest of Troina, a small town of strategic importance to the outcome of the fighting in Sicily. In fact, the town is located on a hill that dominates the main road leading to Messina, and the German army wanted at all costs to hold that position to permit its troops to retreat and embark for the Italian continent, moving the battlefront farther north.

2. Charles Poletti (1903–2002), shown here at the center of the photograph during a reception in Palermo in 1944, performed an important role during the occupation of Sicily by the American liberation troops. He was well trained as a politician, but what distinguished him and led to his being nominated colonel in charge of the civil affairs for the U.S. Army, therefore governor of Sicily, was a more practical consideration: the greater willingness of most of the island's population to deal with an official of Italian origin, even though he was from the north of the country, his father being from Novara and his mother from Varese. During the years following the end of the war Poletti always denied any special relationship with the Mafia, but he associated with Vito Genovese, Lucky Luciano, and Calogero Vizzini, among others. Poletti died at the age of ninety-nine and was buried in the Calkins Cemetery of Elizabethtown, New York; he took with him many secrets that may never be revealed.

3–4. From the report of the Anti-Mafia Commission presented to the chamber on February 4, 1976: "Shortly before the Anglo-American landings in Sicily, numerous elements of the American army were sent to the island to make contact with certain people and to awaken feelings favorable to the Allies in the population. In fact, once the occupation of Sicily had been decided at Casablanca, the Naval Intelligence Service organized a special squad (the Target Section), giving it the task of collecting information necessary for the purposes of the landing as well as the 'psychological preparation' of Sicily. Thus a dense informative network was set up, which established invaluable connections with Sicily, and an increasingly large number of collaborators and informers was sent to the island."

The description fits that of Vito Genovese only partially. He'd already been in Italy a few years, and given the scope of his criminal career it seems obvious that in supporting the needs of the Allies he looked after his own interests as well as those of his friends. At above right he is portrayed in a mugshot taken in 1934 by the New York City Police Department; to the right he appears wearing the uniform of the American army beside the bandit Salvatore Giuliano.

Vito Genovese was born in Tufino, in the province of Naples, on November 27, 1897. He arrived in the United States in 1913 and settled with his family in New York's Little Italy. He was around twenty when he met Lucky Luciano and they established a friendship that lasted his entire life. Involved in the elimination of Masseria and Maranzano, he was forced to flee to Italy in 1937, sought for the murder of another mafioso. In Italy he was first an enthusiastic supporter of Mussolini's government, then he sided with the invasion troops and served as an interpreter, a role that permitted him to move about undisturbed and, most of all, to profitably keep busy with the black market and contraband.

5. The story of Calogero Vizzini begins on July 24, 1877, the day of his birth to a peasant family of Villalba, a small town of four thousand souls not far from Caltanisetta. In the absence of effective state control, the idea gradually emerged that an alternative structure, an organization attentive to local needs, could make up for the central deficiencies. Vizzini rapidly became the boss of Villalba and the nearby territories, providing stability and security by means of a regime that did not disdain violence and extortion.

His power grew until the arrival of the fascist regime and the mission to Sicily of the prefect Cesare Mori, who sent him into confine-ment at Chianciano, although that did not prevent the boss from carrying on his business affairs.

The support the Mafia provided to the invasion of Sicily is still the subject of debate. While there is no proof that the Allies knowingly made use of the Mafia network, it is clear that the Mafia was able to exploit every useful opportunity. One such opportunity was offered by the Allied Military Government of Occupied Territories (AMGOT), which entrusted the political positions occupied by members of the Mussolini regime to replacements of proven antifascist leaning. So it happened that in 1943 Calogero Vizzini became the mayor of Villalba.

6. This photo of Salvatore Giuliano has much to say. It speaks of a man between twenty and thirty years old, confident and much aware of his own appeal, his hands hooked in his belt, his hair shiny with cream—a romantic bandit like Bonnie and Clyde or Robin Hood, capable of combating the arrogance of the rich while defending the poor Sicilian peasants oppressed by a cruel and distant state. Too bad things were not that way and that Salvatore, known as Turiddu, was no hero, as indicated by the dozens of victims he left behind in the dark period that runs from the Second World War to the early postwar years.

He was born in Montelepre on November 16, 1922, fourth child of Salvatore and Maria. A normal child, he helped his father work in the fields while earning his primary school certificate. The war brought a load of miseries that were hard to bear, and to make things easier at home Turiddu got involved in the black market. On September 2, 1943, while illegally transporting several sacks of flour, he was intercepted by a patrol. Although wounded, Giuliano managed to defend himself, killing a *carabiniere*. This gesture marked the beginning of his career as a bandit. Salvatore gathered about fifteen others around him, a small army of outcasts and delinquents, and with them he committed thefts and armed robberies.

7–8. Turiddu's criminal career was impressive, as reflected in dramatic numbers: 149 killed, among them 42 civilians; more than 170 attempted murders; and almost 50 kidnappings (the photo at right shows one of the victims; the photo below shows a member of the gang killed by law officers).

Such activity couldn't help but attract the attention of the Mafia, and Calogero Vizzini seems to have made contact with the bandit; so did the Sicilian Independence Movement (MIS), which was so eager to have him as a member they offered him the rank of colonel in the EVIS or volunteer army, the movement's armed branch.

At first Giuliano was unable to make up his mind, but eventually he accepted, asking in exchange for the cancellation of all the crimes he'd committed up to then. Even so, certain documents found recently suggest that in the period between 1944 and 1947 Giuliano was also courted by neofascist movements, from Decima Mas to the Squadre Azione Mussolini, as well as by the American secret services, concerned about the possible rise to power of parties on the left.

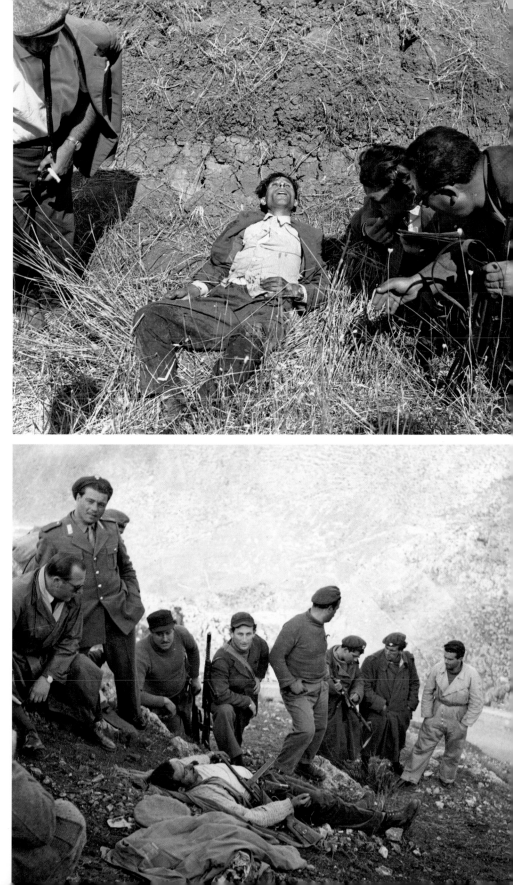

IL 1° MAGGIO 1947
QUI SULLA PIETRA DI BARBATO
CELEBRANDO LA FESTA DEL LAVORO
E LA VITTORIA DEL 20 APRILE
IL POPOLO DI PIANA DEGLI ALBANESI
DI S. GIUSEPPE DI S CIPIRRELLO
SU UOMINI DONNE BAMBINI
SI ABBATTÉ CON FEROCE BARBARIE
IL PIOMBO DELLA MAFIA E DEGLI AGRARI

9. May 1, 1947, saw the celebration of labor day. Under the fascist regime the holiday had been moved to April, but the people who gathered at the mountain pass of Portella della Ginestra for the celebration, arriving from Piana degli Albanesi, Altofonte, and San Giuseppe Jato, came for something more. They also came to protest against the large landowners, who had not given up a fraction of their holdings, and to celebrate the recent elections, those of the regional assembly, held on April 20, in which the Blocco del Popolo, the Socialist-Communist coalition, had defeated the Christian Democrats. That day's assembly was supposed to be led by Girolamo Li Causi, an antifascist who had paid for his political stance with hard years of imprisonment. But another engagement kept the politician away, and addressing the assembly fell to the trade unionist Giacomo Schirò, secretary of the San Giuseppe Jato local branch of the Socialist Party.

No sooner had he begun speaking, at nine-thirty that morning, than the sound of gunfire and cries of pain drowned out everything. In the end it was a slaughter, with eleven dead, including two children, and twenty-seven wounded. There were few doubts it was Giuliano's gang that opened fire, but he claimed he never would have given the order to fire into an unarmed crowd. There is then a disturbing detail: ballistic examination of the bullets found at the scene or extracted from the bodies reveals that the weapons fired were not those used by the bandits but those usually possessed by Decima Mas (a commando unit created during the fascist regime).

10. The trial for the events of Portella della Ginesta ended five years after the slaughter, on May 3, 1952. More than two hundred hearings were required to reach a sentence, and the verdict was severe for twelve men from Giuliano's gang, found guilty of the material execution of the murders and thus sentenced to life imprisonment; as for the instigators, even today the truth is still far from revealed. Perhaps Gaspare Pisciotta, Giuliano's lieutenant who claimed to have killed him, could have added something. Perhaps. In any case, a generous dose of strychnine brought a drastic end to the question of whether or not he would ever reveal what he knew.

11. At nine-thirty on the night of August 19, 1949, a tremendous explosion rocked the buildings of Passo di Rigano, a small suburb outside Palermo. Salvatore Giuliano and his men were responsible for the slaughter, carrying out a plan articulated in three phases that took the lives of seven young *carabinieri*, with another ten wounded.

First the barracks of Bellolampo seemed to come under attack, attracting a contingent of *carabinieri* from Palermo. As the unit returned from this faked attack the convoy of vehicles passed over a powerful antitank mine that had been positioned on the shoulder of the road and that exploded at the passage of the column. The members of the armed forces who then rushed to the aid of their stricken comrades came under fire from bandits positioned to ambush them. The funeral took place in a Palermo scarred by yet another episode in the war ignited by the power struggle between criminal gangs, separatists, landowners, and Mafia bosses.

12. *Crimen* was a weekly news magazine that satisfied the public's morbid interest in crime and criminals. The cover shown here bears the image of the bandit Salvatore Pecoraro, killed by the *carabinieri* under Colonel Luca of Bellolampo. Above the body is the warning "Salvatore Giuliano, attention!" Following the slaughter at Portella and the attack at Bellolampo, Salvatore Giuliano was a hunted man, an awkward ally now for everyone, a delinquent to avoid.

Even the state got involved, apparently for once forced to react. Ugo Luca, late of the secret services, was put in command of a special force to fight bandits, the Comando Forze Repressione Banditismo (CFRD). *Crimen's* call to Giuliano to give himself up was sound advice, which Giuliano failed to heed, paying with his life.

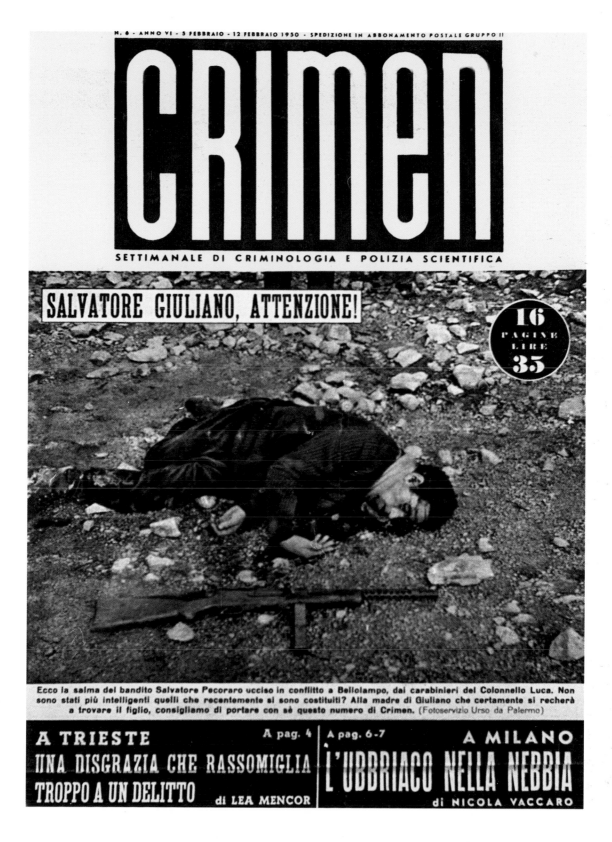

N. 6 - ANNO VI - 5 FEBBRAIO - 12 FEBBRAIO 1950 - SPEDIZIONE IN ABBONAMENTO POSTALE GRUPPO II

CRIMEN

SETTIMANALE DI CRIMINOLOGIA E POLIZIA SCIENTIFICA

SALVATORE GIULIANO, ATTENZIONE!

16 PAGINE LIRE **35**

Ecco la salma del bandito Salvatore Pecoraro ucciso in conflitto a Bellolampo, dai carabinieri del Colonnello Luca. Non sono stati più intelligenti quelli che recentemente si sono costituiti? Alla madre di Giuliano che certamente si recherà a trovare il figlio, consigliamo di portare con sé questo numero di Crimen. (Fotoservizio Urso da Palermo)

A TRIESTE
A pag. 4
UNA DISGRAZIA CHE RASSOMIGLIA TROPPO A UN DELITTO
di LEA MENCOR

A pag. 6-7
A MILANO
L'UBBRIACO NELLA NEBBIA
di NICOLA VACCARO

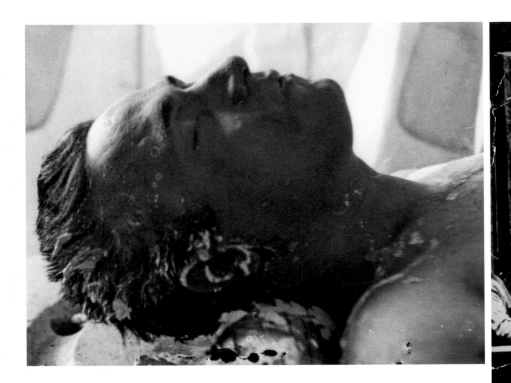

13–14. There are many versions of the death of Salvatore Giuliano, killed July 5, 1950. The only certainty is that the scene, as presented to the public and immortalized in the photographs released by the press, was in reality a theatrical production.

The official version speaks of a gunfight between *carabinieri* and the bandit, who was then mortally wounded in the courtyard of the home of the lawyer Gregorio Di Maria at Castelvetrano.

Unfortunately, the distribution of the wounds, and of the blood that flowed from them, indicate that Giuliano was killed elsewhere and was already dead when positioned in the courtyard.

There are even those who hold that the body does not belong to the bandit but to a double, and that in fact Giuliano fled overseas under a false name, having covered his tracks in Spain, or Algeria, without ever returning to Italy.

15. Gaspare Pisciotta (1924–1954) was born in Montelepre, like Giuliano, and the two were childhood friends. The war divided them, and while Salvatore evaded the draft Gaspare left home as a soldier and was captured, released only in 1945. From then on their destinies were again joined, such that Pisciotta was one of the men involved in the slaughter at Portella. He was taken into custody, and during the trial hearings he declared that the people who'd ordered the attack had been reputable men and princes, deputies and ministers. These weighty charges, perhaps not completely cut out of whole cloth, did not result in investigations.

Then, in April 1951, came the revelation about Giuliano's death, that it had been him, Gaspare Pisciotta, who had killed his friend and boss. He had already betrayed him in exchange for immunity and for a large sum of money, and he'd been ready to hand him over to Colonel Luca by drawing him into an ambush. Then the fear had come over him that Giuliano knew everything, and taking advantage of a moment in which Giuliano was asleep he had shot him in the back. The scene in the courtyard of the lawyer Di Maria had been cunningly constructed, with the body of the bandit already beginning to stiffen.

16. Even though four years had passed since the death of Salvatore Giuliano and seven since the massacre of May 1, 1947, perhaps Gaspare Pisciotta still had something to say. Or perhaps he had nothing left to say and the whole thing was just a bluff.

Without doubt, he was afraid of prison and didn't want to share a cell with anyone. He had no faith in the food provided by the prison administration so his mother prepared his meals, cooking for him every day. On February 9, 1954, Pisciotta dissolved a vitamin preparation pill in his coffee cup. A few minutes later he was on the floor, suffering searing pains in his stomach. He was taken to the infirmary, as seen in this photo, and put on a drip. Forty minutes later his heart stopped beating, a result of the effects of acute strychnine poisoning. Whoever decided to close Pisciotta's mouth forever got away with it: no one was ever officially investigated.

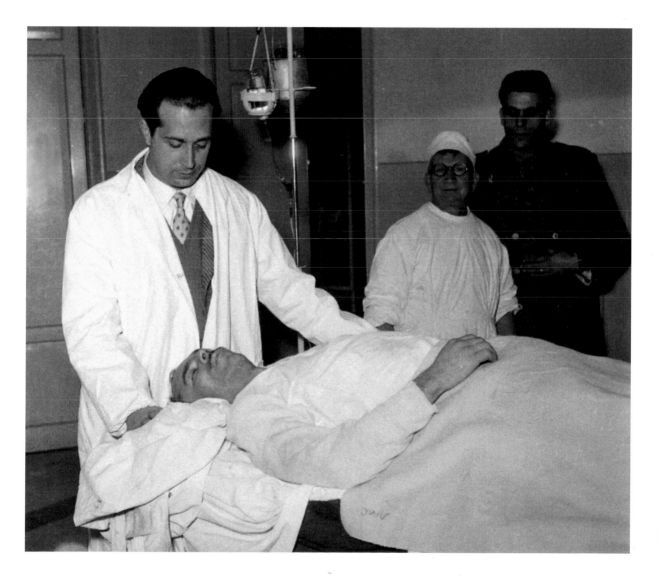

17. This photograph presents one of the last demonstrations of the Sicilian Independence Movement (MIS), which fought a political battle for the secession of the island from 1943 to 1951. The movement began with Italy's surrender on September 8, 1942, which Sicilians saw as another demonstration of the government's detachment from the reality of Sicily. The leader of the movement, who to a certain degree took romantic inspiration from the events of the Sicilian Vespers, was Andrea Finocchiaro Aprile (1878–1964), who was forever tied to the fate of MIS. After discreet success in the elections for the constituent assembly in 1946 and a confirmation in the regionals of the next year, in 1951 the movement did not win a single seat in the regionals and dissolved soon after.

18. Involved with the Allies during the liberation of Sicily, capable of winking at the separatist movement only to then swerve away toward the Christian Democrats when he understood Finocchiaro Aprile did not have a great future, Calogero Vizzini—Don Calò or, to his friends, *'u zu Calò*—was a perfect example of the old-style Mafia boss.

In the years 1949 and 1950 he was often seen in the company of another heavy hitter, Lucky Luciano, born Salvatore Lucania and expelled from the United States, where he had been charged for involvement in a prostitution ring.

The bosses talked and perhaps they did some business together, things related to the drug traffic, but there is no sure proof. When Vizzini died, on July 12, 1954, thousands paid him tribute. In the photo showing the cortege one can see, among many others, Don Francesco Paolo Bontate of Palermo, better known as Don Paolino Bonta, first on the left and father of Stefano, future boss. There is also (near the center, holding a cord tied to the coffin) Don Giuseppe Genco Russo of Mussomeli, who collected Vizzini's inheritance.

The sign that friends attached to the door of the church of Villalba, where the funeral Mass was celebrated, read, "Calogero Vizzini, with the skill of a genius, raised the fate of a distinguished family. Wise and dynamic, never tired, he gave well-being to the workers of the land and the sulfur mines, always acting for good and making a good name for himself in Italy and elsewhere. Great in the face of persecution, even greater facing defeat, he never lost his smile, and today, returned to the peace of Christ in the majesty of death. From all his friends and even from his adversaries, he receives the most beautiful testimonial: he was a gentleman."

19–20. At the time of the funeral of Don Calò, experts in Mafia affairs already knew his heir would be Giuseppe Genco Russo, called *zu Peppi Jencu*. This photograph provides proof, showing him standing beside the coffin striking a pose that is an ancient emblem indicating the line of succession. Genco Russo was born into a very poor family in Mussomeli, a town to which he remained tied all his life, on January 26, 1893. His violent and unscrupulous character soon facilitated his ascent to a man of honor. He came by much of his power through the role he played as mediator between rich landowners and peasants, and although he was responsible for an incredible number of crimes, from extortion to murder, in actual fact he was never once arrested. His Mafia career followed a route parallel to Vizzini's and, in fact, the two were considered the most typical figures of the early Mafia, heirs to a medieval epoch of large landowners.

With the end of the Second World War Genco Russo moved more decidedly toward politics, even performing the role of town councilor in Mussomeli within the ranks of the Christian Democratic party. In October 1957 he took part in the historic meeting of Italian and American bosses held in the Grand Hotel des Palmes in Palermo along with Salvatore Greco, Angelo La Barbera, Gaetano Badalamenti, Tommaso Buscetta, and the Americans Joe Bonanno, Lucky Luciano, and Carmine Galante.

The First Mafia War altered the balance, and things changed, with the first anti-Mafia efforts, and Genco Russo ended up sentenced to five years of confinement. This was a period of decline, as indicated by the photograph opposite, in which, an ailing man, Russo grips the arm of a companion. With him the time of the rural Mafia ended, beginning the epoch of the construction industry, contraband, and finally drug traffic. *Zu Peppi Jencu* died in bed on March 18, 1976, at the age of eighty-three.

21–22. Expropriate the arable land, compensate the large landowners for it, or not, then redistribute the land to the peasants who have no property, and doing so for free or at prices with the easiest terms. Such, in synthesis, was the idea of agrarian reform, always a problem in Sicily. Even Garibaldi, during the expedition of the Thousand, had converted the peasant masses to his cause, enticing them with the promise of reform of the landowners. But

then "the hero of the two worlds" left, leaving behind Nino Bixio to repress the movement of peasant insurrection against the land barons. A few years later it was the turn of the peasant leagues (*Fasci Siciliani*), once again repressed by the central government, this time following the orders of Francesco Crispi. But December 27, 1950, was the day of the change, the day of the agrarian reform bill in Sicily, which has passed into history as the Milazzo

law, after the name of its principal promoter, Silvio Milazzo. Many aspects of the law made it one of the most advanced reform measures ever carried out in Italy; land was expropriated from landowners, then divided into lots and assigned to all those in possession of the qualifications to take part, with a limitation of 150 hectares put on property. Despite the initial enthusiasm the battle of the peasants against the gabellotti (who leased land from the

big landowners) and the Mafia had not been won.

The Agency for Agrarian Reform in Sicily (ERAS) was soon transformed into a gigantic bureaucratic machine, with extremely slow response times, and the Mafia did not stand by and watch, placing some of its outstanding men in strategic positions. An example of this is the position of consultant entrusted to Giuseppe Genco Russo, boss of Mussomeli.

ENTE PER LA RIFORMA AGRARIA
IN SICILIA

LOTTO N. 15

23. The original caption for this image, taken during the fifties in Palermo, reads: "Fruit and vegetable market, site of Mafia murders, deals, and traffic in the immediate postwar period." This story begins during the nineteenth century with the expansion of the areas that faced Palermo's Conca d'Oro. This development was financed by the great earnings furnished by citrus fruits, with commerce entrusted to ships that took lemons throughout the world but most of all to the United States.

Even today it is not uncommon to read of police operations carried out to intercept Mafia organizations that collect protection money from the merchants and from the truck drivers that move fruit and vegetables, resulting in an increase in prices.

24–25. Michele Navarra (1905–1958) stands out from those encountered up to now. He grew up in a well-to-do family and received an excellent education, including, in 1929, a degree in medicine. His association with the Cosa Nostra began in the forties, and during the postwar period Navarra became the unquestioned boss of the Corleone family. This didn't prevent him from continuing to practice the profession of medicine, and indeed he exploited his position to approach influential politicians and to obtain important assignments.

At that point he felt sure enough of himself to get involved in one of the most despicable crimes in Mafia history. Annoyed by the growing success of the trade unionist Placido Rizzotto, Navarra ordered his elimination, entrusting the chore to the young picciotto Luciano Liggio.

Unfortunately, a thirteen-year-old boy, Giuseppe Letizia, witnessed the crime. In a state of shock he ran to report to the *carabinieri*, who took him to the hospital and handed him over to be treated by Dr. Navarra. Soon enough a lethal injection put an end to the young boy.

Over the years, however, things didn't go well between Navarra and Liggio; they were two worlds in conflict, the old and the new, with interests that often clashed. The doctor decided to eliminate his student, unaware that the student had by then outgrown his master. Liggio escaped an ambush, and on August 2, 1958, he got his revenge.

At three-thirty in the afternoon Michele Navarra and his colleague Giovanni Russo were returning home after a day's work in the hospital. They were struck by a fusillade of bullets—at least two hundred were counted—that killed both the boss and his innocent traveling companion on the spot. The double homicide cost Liggio the sentence of life in prison and marked the beginning of the ascent of the Corleone clan.

26. Francesco Coppola (opposite) was born in Partinico, Sicily, in 1899, and like many others he was forced to immigrate, first to New York then to Kansas City, Missouri. The American police were on to him, well aware they were dealing with a cunning criminal, and in 1948 a court issued an expulsion decree. In the meantime Francesco had become Frank "Three Fingers" as the result of an on-the-job accident: during a bank heist his hand got caught in a teller's window, and rather than risk capture he took a knife out of his pocket and freed himself with a single clean cut.

He returned to Partitico, made friends with people of importance, then moved to Pomezia, near Rome, transforming it into the nerve center of drug traffic on the Marseilles–Palermo–New York route. It was no secret that Frank Three Fingers was behind everything, but no one ever managed to catch him. He died of a heart attack on May 10, 1982.

27. Luciano, or Lucianeddu, Leggio (above), became Liggio to everyone as the result of a transcription error made on several court documents during the sixties. Which is nothing more than an anecdote and certainly nothing with an influence on his criminal career, which began very early. He was born on January 6, 1925, and by the time Michele Navarra took him on in 1945 he already had a fair number of crimes to his name, including murder. The murder of Placido Rizzotto on March 10, 1948, drew the attention of the police to him and indeed the suspicions were so many that he ended up behind bars for nearly two years. But the attempt to incriminate him failed, in part because not a single witness could be found ready to come forward. Having eliminated the competition of Michele Navarra, Liggio was ready to control the richest markets in nearby Palermo.

28. The photo of the arrest of Lucianeddu bears the date of May 14, 1964. The boss was surprised by a group of *carabinieri* under the command of Lieutenant Colonel Ignazio Milillo. Liggio's face is swollen and he leans on a cane, claiming to be old and infirm. In reality he was only thirty-nine, and many more chapters of his life remained to be written in blood.

29–30. These two photos, from ID cards that date to the fifties, show two young men, two accomplices, two cruel criminals joined by their shared membership in the Corleone clan.

Salvatore Riina (above) was born in Corleone on November 16, 1930; when he was thirteen, his father and brother Francesco lost their lives while handling an unexploded American bomb, an event that changed Salvatore's life. As the eldest son, it was up to him to support the family, and he took the easy route to earnings, that of crime. He was nineteen when he committed his first homicide. *Totò 'u Curtu* (the "Short One"), as he was called because of his low stature, met Luciano Liggio and put himself in his service, bringing along his childhood friends Bernardo Provenzano (right) and Calogero Bagarella. Provenzano (born in 1933) grew up in a very poor family in Corleone, the third of seven children. He had no childhood; his early years were spent working in the fields and, as for school, he barely learned to read and write. But he excelled at one thing: he was a cruel and bloody killer, so much so his boss, Luciano Liggio, declared that Provenzano "shoots like a god." The nickname he was given drew only more attention to his skills: Binu *'u Tratturi*, Bernardo "the Tractor," for the violence and skill with which he mowed down his enemies.

6 The Corleonesi Arrive

Victims, Widows, and the First Mafia War

Two important events took place in Sicily during the 1950s: Don Calogero Vizzini died, in 1954, and was succeeded by Giuseppe Genco Russo, and people began speaking more and more often of Corleone and the Corleonesi.

Corleone is a small city about fifty miles from Palermo. It has distant origins and, in addition to ancient settlements of Sicanians and other early inhabitants and the Punic Wars, its history includes several facts worthy of being cited, such as the role it played alongside Palermo in driving the Angevins out of Sicily during the Sicilian Vespers. In fact, there is no important battle on the island that did not find Corleonesi involved in the front ranks, so much so that Charles V, visiting the city in 1556, conferred on it the title *Animosa civitas* ("valiant town").

Three centuries later, in 1860, we find that Garibaldi made a "diversion" to Corleone and only afterward directed his attack on the conquest of Palermo; and at the end of the century the town had the heroic Bernardino Verro and the revolutionary peasant leagues.

Around the middle of the twentieth century the Corleonesi was an emerging family but still did not dominate the criminal scene in Sicily; it was commanded by the doctor Michele Navarra, called *'u Patri Nostru* ("Our Father"), an indication of the timorous veneration he inspired.

Cynical and heartless, ready to murder a young boy only because he had witnessed a murder, Navarra was a man of honor tied to the old world of godfathers. He was nothing like the new generation of mafiosi in his service, those whom some called the *viddani* ("the peasants"), as a criticism of their uncouth ways; the oldest was called Luciano Liggio, born in 1925, and behind him were the younger Totò Riina, Bernardo Provenzano, Calogero Bagarella, and then Calogero's brother, Leoluca Bagarella, who was still a boy.

The *viddani* had difficulties accepting the rules and discipline imposed by Dr. Navarra. They wanted more money, more power, more autonomy. This was something that had been seen in the past, and the godfather had no choice but to eliminate his own men since family obedience was the first rule. And as had already happened in the history of the Mafia, the doctor's attempt to free himself of Liggio and his men failed, leading to immediate retaliation.

The internal feud in the clan did not stop at the assassination of Navarra, killed on the afternoon of August 2, 1958, and Liggio's ascent to power proved unstoppable, with blasts of *lupara* and Kalashnikov; the *mattanza* ("killing") of Corleone left at least seventy adversaries on the field and an indefinite number of widows and orphans.

Meanwhile, another event of great importance was about to take place: the so-called First Mafia War. This was set off in 1962 by a dispute over a shipment of drugs destined for New York, a shipment financed by the La Barbera brothers, Angelo and Salvatore, both of the Greco clan of Ciaculli.

When the merchandise reached the Sicilian coast from Egypt, it fell to the man of honor Calcedonia Di Pisa to see that it was embarked without problems on the ship *Saturnia*, en route to the United States. But when the *cugini* in Brooklyn counted the packets, they found the numbers did not add up. Someone had swindled them.

Suspicion fell first on one of the workers on the *Saturnia*, to whom Di Pisa had entrusted the drugs, but the man knew nothing and had nothing to add despite the torture he was subjected to. It was inevitable that suspicion then fell on Di Pisa himself.

He defended himself, and energetically, and the case merited discussion at the uppermost rungs of the Cosa Nostra, among those who formed the Commission. Going against the opinion of the La Barbera brothers, Di Pisa was believed innocent, although that failed to save his life: on December 26, 1962, he was killed while entering a smoke shop in Camporeale, and with him, in the coming days, fell other members of his family, on the orders of Angelo and Salvatore.

This set off almost immediate retaliation, and on January 17, 1963, Salvatore La Barbera disappeared forever, victim of a *lupara bianca* (meaning leaving no corpse). Angelo too disappeared, but only as a precaution, and on February 13 a car exploded, destroying the home of Salvatore Greco, without, however, harming the Ciaculli boss.

Only one month later two hit men in a Fiat 600 opened fire on the Pescheria Impero, in Palermo's Via Empedocle Restivo, where Angelo La Barbera was believed to be. Two died from the shots fired by the killers and another two were wounded, among them an innocent passerby. But Angelo came out of it unscathed. The next move was up to him, and the person to die was an ally of the Grecos, the boss of Cinisi Cesare Manzella.

On the morning of May 25, 1963, in Viale Regina Giovanna in Milan, two cars pulled alongside La Barbera's and opened fire. He was hit six times but survived. The act aroused public indignation since the Mafia had never before dared transform a residential zone of the city into a scene from a Wild West shoot-out, with the risk of harming dozens of innocent citizens.

This was nothing like what happened on June 30, 1963, when a telephone call arrived at the Palermo police headquarters: there was a car abandoned in the open countryside. The car exploded, killing seven men of the police force in an attack that came to be called the Ciaculli massacre and that filled the front pages of newspapers.

For some people this marked the end of the first war, while others put the closing point a little later, involving the Corleonesi.

During the family fighting, Liggio and his men stayed in the background, allying themselves with the La Barbera clan, a marginal position, although they had to answer to the law for the murders of the *mattanza*. They were acquitted in June 1969 on the basis of insufficient evidence and thus were able to dedicate all of their energy to the conquest of power.

The Viale Lazio bloodbath, on December 10, 1969, marked the end of the Mafia conflict and also the beginning of its uncontested ascent.

124

1. A crowd follows two women, a crowd of men. Some help support the youngest, who seems on the point of fainting. Others try to restrain the older since the look on her face speaks pain but most of all anger. The arm thrust forward is particularly worrisome for its indication of anger that might lead her to say something when she would do better to remain silent. Mafia women, always depositories of tradition, ready to do what is necessary to provide serenity and stability to the family, are even more conservative than their husbands and sons.

2. Often those who die are not the bosses of rival families, the armed ringleaders surrounded by young men ready to shoot for them. Death also comes to the few who refuse to bow their heads, who will not give in to a demand, whether for a favor or the payment of a *pizzo* (protection money). For them there is no funeral with flowers and a procession. They are not called Don Calò. For them there is only a cart for the last journey and a widow holding on to the coffin and weeping for a murdered husband.

3. The photo presents a wake at home when everyone stops by to offer their condolences, even those who knew what was going to happen and did nothing to prevent it, or even approved what was done because the victim had been warned and still did not have the common sense to understand. The faces of the family members show the full range of emotions, from the desperation of the widow to the sadness, incredulity, and fear in the eyes of the children. The drama is not only in the loss of a husband or father but in a future devoid of certainty.

4. On August 9, 1952, Giovanni Passatempo and Emanuele Di Maria were killed along the road leading to Monreale. Both of them were bandits in some way related to Salvatore Giuliano, but unlike the stories immediately in circulation they did not fall in a shoot-out with the *carabinieri*. This is made clear by a lieutenant of the *carabinieri*, who points out that the men were killed with a machine gun and a double-barreled shotgun, a small detail that is also certain proof.

Two days before the double homicide Gaspare Pisciotta had been interrogated on the accusations he had directed at Mario Scelba, and other politicians, in the course of the trial at Viterbo. But he preferred to be silent. He would speak, he claimed, only if a parliamentary commission were instituted to look into all the events of Salvatore Giuliano, including the slaughter at Portella and the circumstances of Giuliano's death.

5. This photograph is from the early fifties and the scene of the crime is the countryside around Corleone. Little else is known of the photo except that it was a case of wife killing. It was easier to imagine that the victim had brought dishonor to a family than to imagine a connection with the world of the Mafia. Women, true depositories of the tradition of *omertà*, are difficult to find fault with or challenge. And if they happen to witness something of which it would be better to remain silent, one can count on their silence.

6. The year was 1956. By then the "Mafia of the markets," also called the "Mafia of the gardens," not only controlled the wholesale market of fruits and vegetables and their distribution among small tradesman, but also was involved in the supply of fertilizers and laborers, the transport of products, and the control of prices at every step of the transaction.

The conquest of the market ordained that on August 23 the decision was made to kill Angelo Galatolo. Four months earlier it had been the turn of his brother Gaetano, called 'un zu Tanu.

7. Salvatore Carnevale had just turned thirty when he was killed. Born in Galati Mamertino on September 23, 1923, he moved to Sciara with his mother and was soon drawn to the Movimento Socialista, demonstrating alongside peasants so that agrarian reform would not remain merely an empty promise. For all his efforts he was arrested and left without a job. But on April 29, 1955, he had a new chance when he was hired by the Albertini quarry. After only fifteen days he had organized a first strike, with the workers demanding an eight-hour day, and he had half the laborers of the quarry with him, crossing their arms as he did. A first warning did not have the desired result, so on May 16, 1955, in the Cozze Secche zone, a hit man wounded him in the side and then followed him and, while blood spread beneath his body, fired two shots into his head.

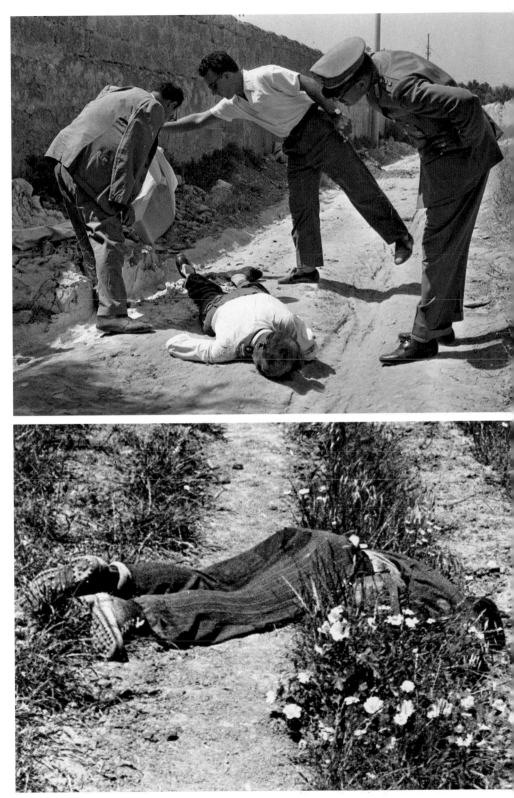

8. Francesca Serio, the mother of Turiddu Carnevale, had a premonition. That night she had a terrible dream and saying good-bye to her son she told him to watch out. When she heard a man had been shot she understood at once and began running toward the quarry. Newspapers told of how a *carabiniere* tried to stop her, telling her it wasn't Salvatore. To which she responded, "Coward, this isn't my son? Those aren't the feet of my son? And those aren't the socks I washed for my son yesterday, which he put on his feet?" The desperate mother had no qualms about pointing her finger at the men who'd killed her son, and the trial that ended in December 1961 seemed to prove her right. The four men accused of the murder of Carnevale were all given life in prison. But the appeals process, which took place in Naples two years later, and then the Court of Cassation (court of final appeal), acquitted all of them.

9. This image, with its powerful impact, presents a woman standing in a courtroom wrapped in a black shawl. To her side is a lawyer, found for her by the journalist Mario Francese, but she seems to have no need, such is the force she has inside herself. This is Serafina Battaglia, the first woman to dare challenge the Mafia. Her story, at least in the beginning, was simple and had already been seen many times in the Sicily dominated by Mafia gangs. Her husband, Stefano Leale, was killed and she dressed herself in widow's weeds and kept her silence; then she talked her son Salvatore into avenging his father's death. The enemies were Vincenzo and Filippo Rimi, bosses of Alcamo, but the son's attempt failed and the inexorable vendetta arrived. Salvatore died in an ambush on January 30, 1962, and Serafina's pain was just too great. She began filling in the judges on all the secrets her husband had told her about before being killed, the business carried on by the clans, the reasons behind many crimes. The moment came in the courtroom when she said, "The mafiosi are little boys. They're tough only around those who are afraid of them, but if you're brave enough to attack them and demolish them, they become cowards. They are not men of honor, nothing but dirt." Serafina Battaglia went around armed, expecting at any moment that someone would try to close her mouth. But there was no need to attract so much attention; it was enough to speak to the right person. For while the first trial of the Rimi brothers ended in their conviction, the court of cassation annulled all of it.

132

10. Pietro Torretta (1912–1975) on the day of his arrest, February 9, 1964. His name, together with those of dozens of mafiosi, ended up in the investigation files collected by Judge Cesare Terranova, who charged him with fourteen homicides. Torretta's history went way back, so far that some believed him to be the son of a certain Francesco cited in the Sangiorgi report drawn up between 1898 and 1900. Tied to Salvatore Giuliano, he became the boss of the Uditore quarter of Palermo and was one of the leaders in the First Mafia War, alongside the La Barbera brothers and an adversary of the clan led by Salvatore Greco, called *Ciaschiteddu*.

11. *Ciaschiteddu*, meaning "little wine jug," is no nickname to brag about, but that did not prevent Salvatore Greco (1912–1978) from becoming one of the most important Mafia bosses of the fifties and sixties, head of the Ciaculli clan. Cousin of the Salvatore Greco called "the Engineer," *Ciaschiteddu* was present at the meeting of the representatives of the Sicilian and American Cosa Nostra held in 1957 in the Grand Hotel des Palmes in Palermo. In fact, he was elected head of the Commission formed on that occasion.

A leading player in the First Mafia War and the Ciaculli massacre, he was forced to flee to Venezuela, then to make contact with the Gambino family in New York. In 1978 he was said to have returned to Italy to side with Gaetano Badalamenti and Salvatore Inzerillo in their struggle against the growing power of the Corleonesi. He died in March 1978 at fifty-five due to complications of cirrhosis of the liver.

12. It was a dumbstruck crowd that followed the coffins. Inside the coffins were the mangled bodies of the victims of the terrible attack that has passed into history as the Ciaculli massacre. Seven men were killed on a summer's day: the *carabinieri* Eugenio Altomare, Silvio Corrao, Marino Fardelli, Mario Malausa, and Calogero Vaccaro, and the soldiers Giorgio Ciacci and Pasquale Nuccio.

On June 30, 1963, a suspicious vehicle was reported, an Alfa Romeo Giulietta abandoned with its doors open. A car bomb, perhaps, so a bomb squad was called in and found a fuse connected to a small bomb and in a short time everything was safe. No one thought of a trap: the true bomb was hidden in the trunk, and the attempt to open it set off a devastating explosion. The peacekeepers were most probably not the target of the bomb but rather the Greco cousins, competing with the La Barbera clan. But even today there is no certainty about who was really behind the slaughter.

13–14–15. There was a two-year difference between Salvatore La Barbera (1922–1963), on the left in the ID photo, and Angelo, his younger brother, portrayed on the right and also opposite while getting off an airplane in handcuffs, dressed in the style of a thirties-era American gangster.

The brothers grew up in Partana Mondello, the quarter to the north of Palermo, and their criminal careers were rapid, with an escalation that went from theft to homicide, from contraband to construction to heroin traffic. Salvatore was part of the first Mafia Commission as capo-mandamento of the family of Porta Nuova, Borgo Vecchio, and Palermo Centro. Affiliated to his clan was a promising youth by the name of Tommaso Buscetta. During the First Mafia War, Salvatore disappeared into thin air, the victim of a *lupara bianca*. Although certain proof has never been found, it seems that Michele Cavataio was behind his elimination. After the Ciaculli massacre Angelo (1924–1975) was involved in the Trial of the 114, so called for the number of defendants. The trial was held at Catanzaro between December 1967 and December 1968. Convicted, Angelo La Barbera was being held in the prison of Perugia when, in 1975, he was attacked and stabbed to death by three other prisoners.

16. The first Anti-Mafia Commission was convened on February 14, 1963, its purpose to "propose the necessary measures to repress the manifestations and to eliminate the causes of the Mafia." The second commission began work in September 1982, in relation to the so-called Rognoni–La Torre law. The current version, related to the sixteenth legislative term, is composed of twenty-five deputies and an equal number of senators and is presided over by the former interior minister Giuseppe Pisanu.

17. Palermo, December 10, 1969: the attack in Viale Lazio was the event that finally put an end to the First Mafia War. Girolamo Moncada had his construction company's offices in Viale Lazio, and Michele Cavataio had his base there. Michele, called the "Cobra," the boss of Acquasanta, was the target of a five-man crew of hit men, among them Bernardo Provenzano, Totò Riina, and Calogero Bagarella. To avoid attracting suspicion they showed up dressed in the stolen uniforms of customs officers, then took out their weapons. Cavataio had time to respond, pulling out a pistol and pointing it at Provenzano, but it was unloaded; Bino 'u Tratturi's gun jammed so he killed Cavataio by bashing in his skull with the butt of a rifle. Five men died that day, including Calogero Bagarella.

6 The Corleonesi Arrive

Lucky Luciano, Carlo Gambino, and the Others

Big Families and Big Bosses

As with the Sicilian Mafia over the course of its history, so too the American model evolved and adapted to changes in the social context, to changes in the sources of income that were easiest to exploit, in the political response, and in the forces of opposition.

With the end of the era of Prohibition, the period that runs from the postwar to the death of Carlo Gambino coincides with that of greatest expansion in the criminal families, but it also represents the period in which, for the first time and in explicit terms, people began talking about a Mafia problem. During these years the leaders of the Gambino family were Vincent Mangano followed by Albert Anastasia and finally Carlo Gambino. The Bonanno clan was dominated by Joseph Bonanno, alias Joe Bananas. Vito Genovese was the boss of the Genovese family, after whom leadership went to Paul Sciacca and to Natale Evola to end with Carmine Galante, killed in 1979. Outstanding godfathers in the Lucchese family were Tommy Gagliano, Gaetano "Tommy Brown" Lucchese, Carmine Tramunti, and Anthony Corallo.

The Colombo family was commanded by Joe Profaci, then Joseph Magliocco, Joe Colombo, Vincenzo Aloi, and finally Carmine Persico.

Far from New York, in Chicago the law was laid down first by Tony Accardo, then Sam Giancana. Speaking of Giancana opens a world of still unresolved mysteries, including presumed ties between the Chicago Outfit and the Kennedy family and the deaths of JFK and Bobby Kennedy, and even earlier to the suspicious death of Marilyn Monroe.

Between great criminal undertakings and clamorous failures, between diplomatic alliances and bloody clashes, the event that marked the period fell on November 14, 1957.

Apalachin is a town about 200 miles from New York City on the banks of the Susquehanna River, not far from the Pennsylvania border. It was in Apalachin that Joseph "Joe the Barber" Barbara, lieutenant of the Buffalo boss Stefano Magaddino, had a splendid estate. In that year, 1957, the Cosa Nostra had many problems to deal with, beginning with the attack that Frank Costello had escaped by a miracle but with a bullet in his head, then the murder of Albert Anastasia, killed in the barbershop of the Park Sheraton Hotel in Manhattan, and finally Vito Genovese and his mania of calling himself the "Boss of the bosses."

It was time for everyone to sit down around a table and reach some kind of agreement, and having discarded the Chicago option the decision was made that the ideal setting for such a meeting was the vast and yet also isolated property belonging to Joseph Barbara.

It happened, however, that on November 13 Sergeant Edgar Croswell and the investigator Vincent Vasisko found themselves in a motel not far off, looking into a case of false checks, and while seeking information they saw Barbara's son come in and ask if there were any rooms free for some friends of the family.

The Barbara family was already at the center of attention of the local police because word was out they were implicated in contraband alcohol. Not to mention that the year before a guy had been stopped coming out of the Apalachin estate in a car: not only was the man driving without a license but his name was Carmine Galante, which turned out to be on the list of the most dangerous criminals in New York. The next day, around noon, Croswell and Vasisko, together with two U.S. Treasury agents, Arthur Huston and Kenneth Brown, set themselves up in an unmarked car in front of the entrance to the estate.

Many had already arrived to take part in the meeting, and others arrived over the coming hours, coming in thirty-odd limousines that filed past the agents. At the top of the agenda for the Mafia meeting was the Genovese question, but other topics of discussion included the business opportunities and drug traffic going to Cuba thanks to the obliging regime of Fulgencio Batista as well as the international sale of drugs.

Croswell and the other men got out of the car and, in uniform, began taking note of the license plates of the parked cars. The effect of this was immediate panic, and the first car that left the space was that of Emanuel Zicari and Dominic Alaimo. Croswell had the foresight to send two of his colleagues to set up a road block a few miles away to avoid having to stop the car nearby. The trick convinced the others that the road was not blocked and that they could get away before the situation got worse. But as soon as they tried they were stopped by the agents, and the first to be stopped was Vito Genovese.

The situation tumbled into chaos, with fifty-odd men of honor, among them Sam Giancana, Tommy Lucchese, Carmine Galante, and Stefano Magaddino, running off into the woods, along the way emptying their pockets of guns and money.

Among the sixty-three stopped, aside from Vito Genovese, there were men of the caliber of Carlo Gambino, Joe Bonanno, Joe Profaci, Paul Castellano; taken to the local police station and interrogated about why they were all in the Barbara home. They answered with the same story: they'd heard that poor Joseph wasn't feeling well and had decided to pay him a courtesy call. It was only by chance that they had all acted on the same sense of compassion and at the same moment.

The action taken by the sergeant and his colleagues may not have led to any indictments, but it did obtain an important result: news of the summit filled the pages of newspapers, and the McClellan committee, a government panel whose chief counsel was Robert Kennedy, shifted its attention from corruption in organized labor to organized crime.

Another result of the Apalachin meeting was that J. Edgar Hoover, director of the FBI, was forced to change his position concerning the Mafia. Before the meeting he'd held that a criminal organization of the Mafia type was nothing more than a journalistic invention. But now he ordered the launching of a new program to learn more about the Cosa Nostra, called the Top Hoodlum Program, getting each FBI office to make a list of its top ten and collect information on them.

Even today the place-name Apalachin evokes the location of the most famous and most disastrous meeting in the history of the Mafia, because on that far-off November 14, 1957, everyone became aware that a "Mafia problem" existed in the United States.

1–2. Without doubt, Luciano was the most farsighted of the Cosa Nostra's godfathers. During the years preceding the Second World War he had formed a commission composed of representatives of the five New York families: Bonanno, Gambino, Colombo, Genovese, and Lucchese. To these could be added the families in Buffalo, Detroit, Kansas City, Los Angeles, and the Chicago Outfit.

As head of the Genovese family, Luciano had Vito Genovese as his underboss, with Frank Costello as consigliere, while Meyer Lansky and Bugsy Siegel, although having no official roles, were always beside him.

District Attorney Thomas E. Dewey got him on the charge of organizing a prostitution racket. He was sent to prison but given early parole and deported to Italy in 1946. But despite restrictions and checks Luciano did not lose his influence, nor did he stop exercising control over criminal traffic, first of all that of drugs.

The photo opposite shows him in 1949 on the train that took him to Sicily. He is shown below a few years later, in November 1954, after a court hearing during which restrictive measures were applied to his activity. Without certain proof, but "suspected of socially dangerous activity," Luciano for two years was required not to leave his home in Naples between the hours of nine at night and seven the next morning.

3. During the last years of his life Lucky Luciano lived with Igea Lissoni, a young dancer at La Scala he'd fallen in love with only to see her die prematurely from a tumor. On January 26, 1962, he had an appointment to meet a film producer interested in making a film about his life. They were supposed to meet at the arrivals gate at the Naples airport of Capodichino. The gangster suddenly fell heavily to the ground, struck by a heart attack. Luciano had only recently passed his sixty-fourth birthday and, despite his origins and the years spent in Italy, his last wishes had been to be buried in the St. John Cemetery in Queens, New York.

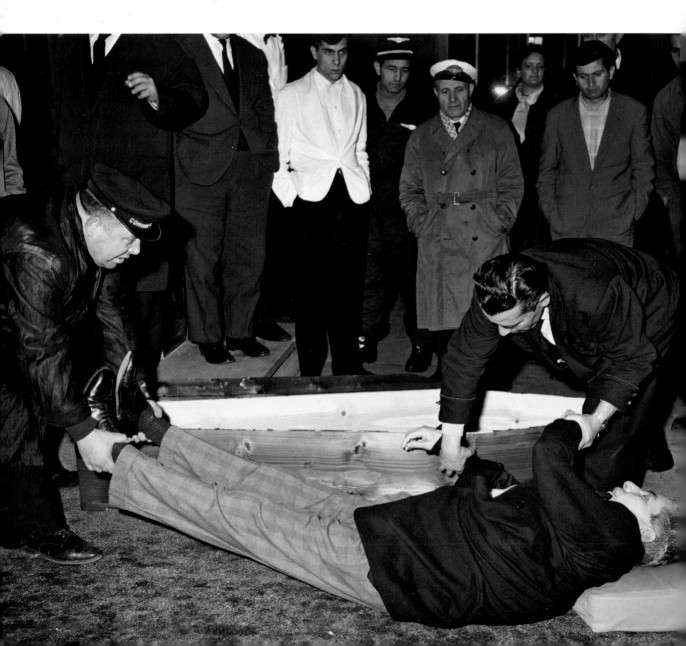

4. His name was Giuseppe Antonio Doto, born in Montemarano in the province of Avellino, near Naples, on November 22, 1902. He illegally entered the United States in 1915. As soon as the authorities learned he'd never obtained American citizenship he was given two options: go to prison or accept extradition and return to Italy. On January 3, 1956, he boarded the SS *Conte Biancamano* and plopped down in a seat between portholes to smile for photographers.

In 1920, always concerned with his personal appeal, he decided to change his name to Joe Adonis. He worked alongside Frankie Yale, took part in the execution of Joe Masseria, but most of all he boasted the respect and consideration of Luciano, who chose him among his most trusted lieutenants.

In Italy he went from Naples to Milan, where he frequented high-fashion locales and nightclubs, always elegant and refined in both manners and dress. Arrested in 1971 and sent to an obligatory residence in the Marches, he was picked up during the course of a police operation on November 26, suddenly took ill during the interrogation, and died of heart failure.

5. Giuseppe Bonanno, nicknamed "Joe Bananas," was born in Castellammare del Golfo on January 18, 1905, and arrived in the United States with his family when he was three. He soon returned to Italy, then moved to Cuba when he was around twenty before returning to the United States, where he obtained citizenship in 1945. As head of one of the most powerful crime families in New York, Joe Bonanno tried to expand his influence in the postwar years, planning the elimination of the bosses of other criminal groups.

In 1964 he disappeared for nineteen months, hostage of the Commission, which managed to get him to retire to private life. The photograph opposite, which shows him together with his lawyer Albert Krieger (on the right), was taken shortly after his reappearance.

Suffering heart problems, Bonanno retired from the scene, moving to Arizona. He lived a final period of glory in 1983 with the publication of his biography, entitled *A Man of Honor*. He died at Tucson on May 11, 2002, at the enviable age of ninety-seven.

6. Carmine Galante, known as "Lilo" for the cigar always stuck in his teeth, was born in New York in 1910. By the late forties he had become one of the leading men of the Bonanno family, after being responsible for several "excellent cadavers," including that of the anti-Mafia and antifascist journalist Carlo Tresca, killed on the orders of Vito Genovese. For the family he was concerned primarily with the drug traffic from Europe and later from Canada. Sentenced to twenty years in 1962 he was visited by psychiatrists who recognized his psychopathic personality, a characteristic he shared with many other brutal criminals.

In 1974, having done his time, Galante tried to take control of the Bonanno family and openly challenged Carlo Gambino. On July 12, 1979, Galante paid for this rude behavior with his life.

7–8. With the end of the Second Mafia War, Vito Genovese was extradited from Italy to the United States, where he was sought to stand trial for murder. The trial ended with a verdict of not guilty because of a series of "inexplicable" accidents that had befallen the state's witnesses. His desire to succeed Luciano brought him into conflict with his old friend Frank Costello. Thomas ("Tommy Ryan") Eboli and Anthony Strollo, among others, sided with Genovese, while Costello could count on Joe Adonis and most of all his underboss, Willie Moretti.

Guarino Moretti, known as "Willie," was killed on October 4, 1951, while eating in Joe's Elbow Room, a restaurant at Cliffside Park, New Jersey (photo opposite). There was no doubt that the three hit men who burst into the place and shot Willie were Genovese men, but Costello decided not to respond immediately to the attack. Then he also lost Joe Adonis, arrested in 1953, and in 1957 his ally Albert Anastasia was killed. So it was that Genovese took the reins of the family, which from then on took his name.

In 1959 he was sentenced to fifteen years for heroin trafficking, but that did not prevent him from continuing to run his business. He suffered greater damage at the hands of one of his own men, Joe Valachi, who turned against him and became the first *pentito* of the Cosa Nostra in the United States. On February 14, 1969, Vito Genovese died in prison from a heart attack at the age of seventy-one.

9. Thomas Eboli (on the right below), known as Tommy Ryan, was born on June 13, 1911. Little is known of his childhood except his passion for boxing. Bodyguard of Lucky Luciano during the thirties and forties, he then flanked Vito Genovese and at Genovese's death took his place as the new boss of the family. On the night of July 16, 1972, Eboli left a girlfriend's apartment in Crown Heights, Brooklyn, and did not have enough time to reach his car, parked nearby. He was struck by five bullets and was dead at the scene. No one was ever charged with the crime, although suspicion fell on Carlo Gambino, who wanted direction of the Genovese family to go to his friend Frank Tieri.

10. Joe Valachi (1903–1971) is certainly an overrated figure in the history of the Cosa Nostra. After a debut in the world of crime as a burglary expert, he joined the Mafia in the thirties, becoming part of the group under Salvatore Maranzano fighting against Joe Massseria.

He then became a soldier in the family of Lucky Luciano and never made it to a higher level of responsibility. His testimony before the Senate's permanent subcommittee on investigations in October 1963 (above) was useful to an understanding of the rules and rituals of the organization and also threw some light on unsolved crimes. But it did not lead to any indictments.

Why did Valachi decide to collaborate with the authorities? Some thought it was the result of a sudden fit of madness, given the fact that many of his family members had displayed more or less serious mental disturbances. Others were willing to believe that he was telling the truth when he said he wanted to get away from a world of inhuman cruelty. But there was also suspicion that the gangster was hoping to make some sort of profit out of his testimony, perhaps obtaining favorable treatment from the government, or the abandonment of the investigation in his part of a murder committed years earlier. During his detention in 1966 Valalchi tried to commit suicide by hanging himself, but he was saved. He died five years later from a heart attack, without having ever gained his freedom.

11–12. Francesco Castiglia, alias Frank Costello, was dubbed "the prime minister of organized crime" during the period of his greatest power. He was born on January 26, 1891, in Lauropoli, a small town in Calabria, and a few years later, together with his mother and brother, he joined his father who in the meantime had opened a small drugstore in Harlem, New York.

He got his education from very particular teachers, such as Ciro Terranova and Piddu Morello. Prohibition brought him into the limelight along with Luciano, Genovese, Adonis, Lansky, and Siegel, and together they took part in the Castellammarese war.

Following the extradition of Lucky Luciano, forced to leave the United States in 1946, Frank became the boss of the family. For a full year, beginning in May 1950, the U.S. Senate conducted an investigation of organized crime headed by its promoter, Tennessee senator Estes Kefauver (1903–1963), shown in his office (opposite). A lineup of criminal types testified before the Kefauver commission, including gangsters, bookies, and pimps, but among all of them it was Costello who conquered the scene. He refused to make use of his Fifth Amendment rights, but when things got rough he simply walked out of the hall. For that reason, in 1952, he was given a sentence of eighteen months. In 1954 the charge was instead that of tax evasion, and he spent eleven months behind bars before being acquitted on appeal. In 1956 new accusations were brought against him that also did not hold up during the appeals process. But Costello's decline was inexorable, and what led him to withdraw was an attempt on his life that he escaped only by a miracle, on May 2, 1957: while coming home with his wife he was attacked by Vincent "Chin" Gigante, a gunman tied to Vito Genovese. Struck by a bullet in the head he never completely recovered. On February 18, 1973, he died of heart failure at the age of eighty-two.

14. Paul John Carbo, born Giovanni Carbo but known as Frankie Carbo, was one of the most important soldiers in the Lucchese family. He was born in New York in 1904 to parents from Agrigento, Sicily, and his nickname says a lot about his temperament: "Mr. Fury." By the end of the thirties Carbo had already collected seventeen arrests and had been accused of at least five murders. He got into the business of organizing boxing matches, becoming known as the "czar of boxing" and profiting from the illegal bets that it is easy to imagine were involved. Even so, boxing also proved to be his ruin. He was accused of fixing fights and in 1961 was sentenced to twenty-five years for conspiracy and extortion against the welterweight champion Don Jordan. Because of his poor health he was allowed to leave prison on parole, and he died in Miami in November 1976. The photo opposite, taken on June 3, 1947, shows Carbo on his way to present himself to the grand jury in New York during an inquest into the boxing racket.

13. Gaetano "Tommy Brown" Lucchese (1899–1967) had a nickname, "Three Fingers," although none of his soldiers would have dared call him by it. He had injured his hand in a machine-shop accident that was certainly not a pleasant memory. He was very young when he fell into the circle of the Reina gang, which ruled the Bronx during the First World War. At the end of the Castellammarese war, with the creation of the Commission, Gaetano Gagliano assumed the place of command and Tommy was his underboss. When the boss died, in 1953, Lucchese assumed command and gave his name to the family. Over the years he forged alliances with the Gambinos and did so in the time-honored style of ancient royalty: Carlo Gambino's son married Lucchese's daughter in a wedding to which more than a thousand guests were invited. If there is anything unique in the Lucchese story, it is the fact that during a career in crime lasting more than forty years he never spent as much as a day in prison. A brain tumor killed him on July 13, 1967. His position as leader of the family was taken by Carmine Tramunti.

15. Carlo Gambino arrived in the United States relatively late in life. Born in Palermo in 1902 he arrived in New York in December of 1921, but for a year he had already been a man of honor, having grown up in a family in which the Mafia was well represented. Waiting for him at his arrival was his uncle Giuseppe Castellano, father of Paul Castellano, who would succeed him on his death. Gambino acquired power that would make him the most feared boss in New York during the years following the Second World War, profiting from the conflict between Albert Anastasia and Vincent Mangano. Once Anastasia had eliminated his adversaries, Gambino began forming alliances with Tommy Lucchese, Vito Genovese, Stefano Magaddino of the Buffalo family, and Angelo Bruno of the Philadelphia family.

In October 1957 a team of hit men sent by Carlo Gambino killed Anastasia, earning him the command of the Mangano family, which from then on was renamed the Gambino family. During the seventies Joseph Colombo and Thomas Eboli were to fall to bullets fired by Gambino hit men.

16–17. Francis Albert Sinatra (1915–1998), with a Sicilian father and a Ligurian mother, never denied knowing members of the Mafia and even had his picture taken in their company. In the photo from January 1978 (above) one sees Paul Castellano, standing at far left, and Carlo Gambino, third from the right. Sinatra always denied any involvement in the business of the Cosa Nostra, and the file made public by the FBI in 1998 did not settle the question of whether this interest in Frank Sinatra was nothing more than a fixation of the bureau's omnipotent director, J. Edgar Hoover. The sole fact of a certain weight imputable to Sinatra dates to the early seventies: induced to make a mistaken investment by a banker, "Old Blue Eyes" was said to have tried to get the lost money back with the energetic assistance of Carlo Gambino and "Crazy Joe" Gallo. But even here there is no certain proof. Just as there is no proof behind the notion that he helped Lucky Luciano launder money or that one of his children was kidnapped by a rival gang of the Gambinos. Despite the conjecturing and badmouthing all that remains is the photo of a group of men posing and smiling for the camera.

18. In 1973 Carlo Gambino's life was struck by tragedy: a gang of low-level hoods kidnapped his nephew Emanuel ("Manny"), planning to demand a ransom, but the young boy died. Gambino's revenge was terrible, tracking down the gang members and killing them one by one. The leader of the gang was killed with two shots to the face inside a crowded Staten Island bar. The shooter was a soldier named John Gotti hoping to be promoted to man of honor. By then old and sick, Gambino chose Paul Castellano as his heir before dying in his home on Long Island on October 15, 1976. The funeral was transformed into a spectacular event. There were about two thousand participants, including some of the leading names in politics and business; behind the hearse flowed an unending stream of dozens of tinted-glass, bulletproof limos.

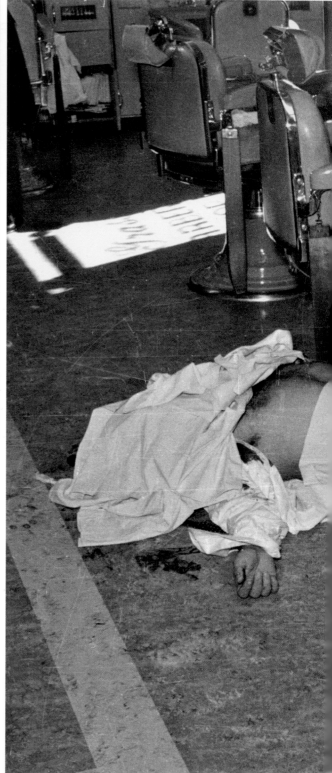

19–20. Like Carlo Gambino, Umberto Anastasio (1902–1957) arrived in the United States somewhat late in life, not before 1919. He immediately changed his name to Albert Anastasia. Albert, or as he was nicknamed the "Mad Hatter," was an ambitious man, and during the fifties he proved himself a little too greedy, so much so that Meyer Lansky and other bosses ordered his elimination. His execution was one of the most spectacular in the history of the Mafia: on October 25, 1957, Anastasia went to his favorite barbershop, in the Park Sheraton Hotel. He had time for a shave; while he was sitting with his face wrapped in a hot towel two hit men came in with their guns drawn and opened fire.

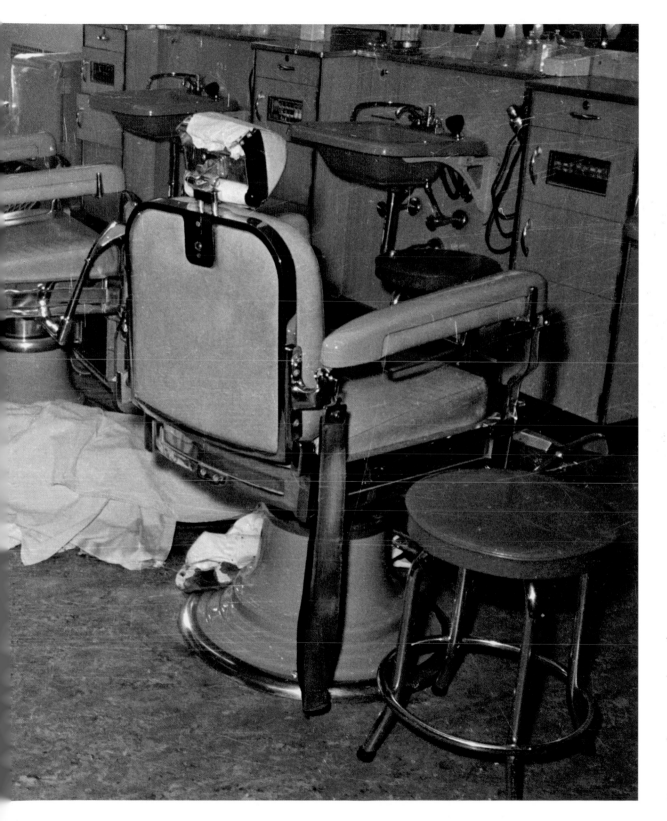

21. Francesco "Frank" Scalice was born in Palermo in 1893 and grew up in the Mafia organization to become the underboss of Albert Anastasia in the years from 1951 to 1957. Like his boss, he too ended up displeasing the Commission. It seems, in fact, that he offered affiliation with the Cosa Nostra in exchange for large sums of money.

On August 17, 1957, Frank was hit by numerous pistol shots in the head and back while standing in a fruit-and-vegetable stand at 2380 Arthur Avenue in the Bronx. His brother Joseph swore he would get revenge without knowing who had ordered the murder. Not long afterward he paid with his life for this unforgivable ignorance.

22. Giuseppe "Joe" Profaci was born in Villabate, in the province of Palermo, on October 2, 1897. In Sicily he was arrested several times for theft and assault, then he immigrated to the United States, going to Chicago in 1921, transferring to New York in 1925. The Castellammarese war saw him in a protected, neutral position, and when Luciano decided in 1931 to reorganize the Cosa Nostra Profaci was chosen to lead one of the five families.

His problems came from the law, first of all, and secondly from his pals. In 1953 the IRS sued him for $2 million in unpaid income taxes. Four years later a crate of oranges he was shipping from Villabrate was found to contain hollow wax oranges filled with heroin. Early in the sixties Profaci had to deal with the challenge of "Crazy Joe" Gallo and his brothers, after which Carlo Gambino and Tommy Lucchese suggested to Profaci that he might want to retire. Profaci refused, convinced that the two bosses only wanted to side with the Gallos, and he kept on fighting until he succumbed to liver cancer, on June 7, 1962. He was succeeded by Joseph Magliocco, who died from natural causes eighteen months later. Next it was the turn of Joseph Colombo, who gave his own name to the family.

23–24. "Crazy Joe" Gallo (1929–1972) is famous in the United States not only for his criminal acts but because Bob Dylan dedicated a song to him on his 1976 album *Desire*. In Dylan's lyrics, Joe is transformed into a criminal with a moral sense, very different from the cruel gangster of reality. Gallo came to the limelight at the end of the fifties when he began to pressure his boss, Joe Profaci, for more power and greater earnings. The result was an internal war destined to end with the death of Profaci.

The photo above, taken October 10, 1961, shows Joe to the left and Larry, his brother, to the right, as they are being taken to prison with a sentence of ten years for extortion. Crazy Joe carried on his business during the time spent behind bars, forming alliances with other inmates, and as soon as he was released, in 1971, he went to war with Joe Colombo, by then in command of the Profaci family. On June 28, during an Italian-American Unity Day rally in Manhattan's Columbus Circle, Gallo's men seriously wounded Colombo (opposite). The boss never regained consciousness and died in 1978.

It didn't take long for the revenge to come, and on April 7, 1972, two killers sent by the Colombo family burst into Umberto's Clam House, a restaurant in Little Italy, where Crazy Joe was celebrating his forty-third birthday with family and friends.

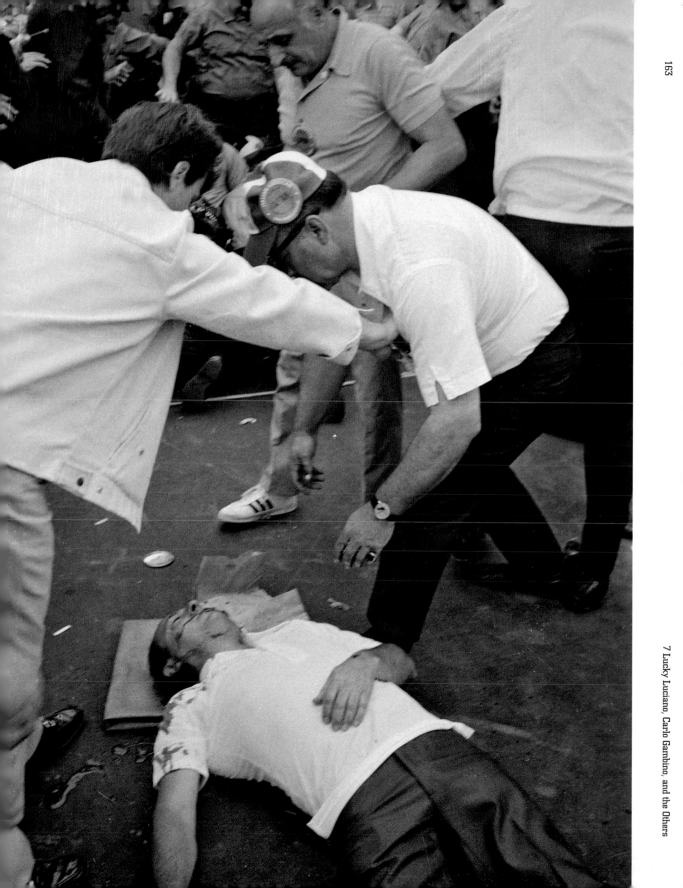

25–26. The photo to the left was taken in 1959, the one opposite five years later; both present views of the San Gennaro Festival in New York City. The festival first took place on September 19, 1926, and since then has grown from a one-day event to eleven consecutive days of celebrations and events. The celebrations begin with the parade in honor of the martyr saint, the patron saint of Naples, and winds its way from Mulberry Street to Mott, between Canal and Houston streets. Since 1996 the festival has been directed by the Figli di San Gennaro, which oversees the collection of offerings for the assistance and educational organizations of Little Italy. During recent years the proceeds from donations have exceeded $1.5 million. Aside from the restaurants and festively lit shops, at least three hundred street vendors crowd the sidewalks, offering gastronomic specialties but also souvenirs, religious curios, and clothes in a sort of big, happy open-air market.

27. Meyer Harris "Mickey" Cohen (1913–1976) was so fond of being the center of attention that he had himself photographed in the middle of newspaper headlines bearing his name as the number-one criminal in Los Angeles.

Born in Brooklyn, New York, he moved to California with his family. During the days of Prohibition he worked for the Chicago Outfit, then alongside Bugsy Siegel, taking his place after his death. In 1950 he was the center of interest of the Kefauver commission, accused of tax evasion and sentenced to four years. A second sentence, for the same reason, was pronounced in 1961. Released from the penitentiary of Atlanta in 1972 he died from natural causes four years later.

28. Johnny Stompanato (1925–1958) had an adventurous life behind him; a veteran of the Second World War, he ended up in China as a government employee, married a Turkish woman, and converted to Islam. When he arrived in Hollywood he did not seek a banal office job. He was paid by Mickey Cohen, one of the best-known gangsters of the era, to serve as his bodyguard. The photo shows the two men walking in the streets of Los Angeles.

29–30. It all began in the spring of 1957 when Johnny Stompanato decided he had to have Lana Turner at all costs. A phone call, the invitation to get a drink, then bouquets of flowers every day. The actress soon learned that her suitor belonged to the world of organized crime, but rather than being put off she seemed drawn in. She liked the way he was aggressive, sometimes even violent, and found that she somehow couldn't do without his overbearing ways, his yells and his slaps. Lana Turner had a daughter, Cheryl (in the picture below being escorted by an agent of the juvenile prison), a timid and insecure adolescent; she was tied to her mother and could not bear seeing her mistreated. On the night of April 4, 1958, she could no longer put up with it. Johnny Stompanato had come by to see Lana because he needed money, having gambled and lost, but this time Turner was resolute: she had no intention of fixing her lover's debts. Cheryl became afraid, ran to the kitchen, and grabbed a carving knife. She stabbed Johnny in the chest and the blade hit the aorta. Before losing consciousness and dying Stompanato managed to say a few words: "My God, Cheryl, what have you done?"

In the courtroom Lana Turner gave one of her very best performances, destroyed by sorrow but at the same time determined to save her daughter from a long imprisonment. "Everything happened so fast . . . I never saw the knife . . . I thought she had hit him in the stomach with her fist. Mr. Stompanato fell forward, then he turned and fell on his back. He had his hands at his throat, suffocating. I ran to him, I raised the pullover and saw the blood . . . he was making terrible sounds in his throat, gasping, terrible sounds." The trial ended with a verdict of justifiable homicide.

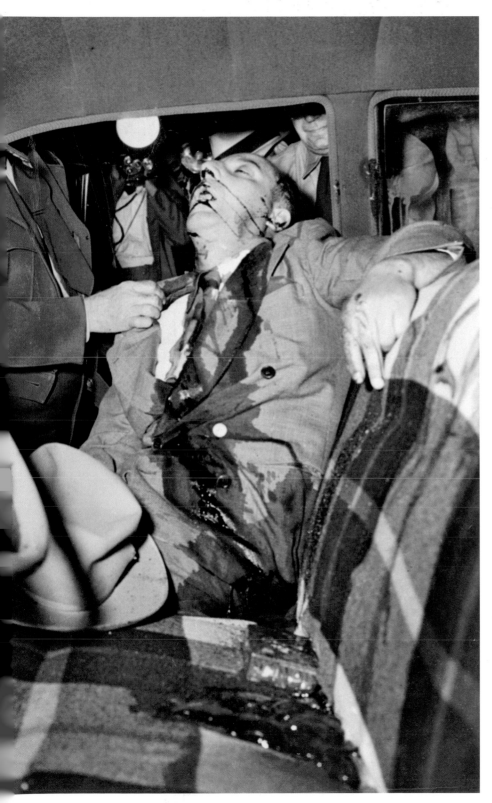

31. Anthony Brancato and Anthony Trombino (the latter shown in the photograph at left) were best known as the "Two Tonys." They came from Kansas City, Missouri, and racked up an impressive number of arrests before committing a fatal error.

On May 28, 1951, they stole $3,500 in cash from the sports betting operation of the Flamingo Hotel in Las Vegas—money from illegal bets. The boss, Jack Dragna, gave the order to eliminate them and entrusted the job to Jimmy Fratiano. He got in contact with the two and drew them into an ambush with the excuse of wanting to discuss a bank heist with them. The bodies of the two men were found on August 6, 1951, on the front seat of a car abandoned near Hollywood Boulevard. The crime remained unsolved for more than twenty-five years, until Jimmy Fratiano entered the Witness Protection Program and it is said he confessed to being responsible for the double murder.

33–34. Antonio Leonardo Accardo, called "Tony" and "Big Tuna" (below), was born in Chicago on April 28, 1906, the son of two immigrants from Castelvetrano, Sicily. He soon became a member of the Chicago Outfit and was named underboss by Paul Ricca, who succeeded Frank Nitti, who in turn had taken the place of Al Capone.

It was Tony who made the organization grow, varying the Outfit's fields of criminal interest and taking over its leadership when Ricca was sentenced to ten years in prison. Pressure from the authorities (the photo was taken in January 1951 on the occasion of his hearing in front of the Senate commission) led him to step aside, leaving the position of family boss to Sam Giancana (opposite) and taking for himself the role of consigliere.

Giancana (1908–1975) was one of the most vicious criminals in Mafia history and also one of the most controversial figures in the history of the Cosa Nostra because of his ties to the world of politics and his possible role in the murders of Marilyn Monroe and the Kennedy brothers. Accardo's decision to entrust command to Giancana seemed to work until Giancana began refusing to share the earnings from the casinos in Central America with the other family members. Giancana was thus replaced by Samuel Battaglia and fled to Mexico; he returned to the United States only in 1975 and was killed on June 19. Accardo, with an incalculable patrimony at his disposition, gradually retired from business, making it possible for him to die in his own bed at the enviable age of eighty-six.

32. Simone Rizzo DeCavalcante, known as Sam the Plumber, shown here with his wife about to take part in their son's wedding in Trenton, New Jersey, on January 9, 1970.

Born April 30, 1913, he was a member of the New Jersey Mafia and the unquestioned boss of the family that bore his name. Around 1960 the FBI investigated his business with a series of wiretaps known as the Goodfella Tapes. The material was not admitted in court, but in 1969 DeCavalcante was incriminated for tax evasion. The boss retired in 1980, his place passing to Giovanni "John the Eagle" Riggi. He died from natural causes in 1997.

35. Exiting the doors of the courtroom in Chicago, in 1964, "Mad Sam" DeStefano shows reporters all his anger; he was probably aware that the trial for criminal association, which would conclude the next year, would end with a heavy sentence.

Born in Illinois in 1909 to Italian parents, DeStefano joined the Chicago Outfit and for the family specialized in loan sharking, protection rackets, and extortion. A sociopathic killer without scruples, DeStefano didn't hesitate about eliminating even his own younger brother at the request of Giancana. The organization itself was disturbed by his sadism, but the bosses put up with him because of the profits he delivered. Even so, on April 14, 1973, DeStefano was killed by a hit man in a garage in Austin, Texas, a crime for which no one was ever charged.

36. The story of the Trafficante family goes way back. At the end of the twenties the first boss of the Tampa Mafia, known for the city of its headquarters, was the Sicilian immigrant Ignazio Antinori. He was succeeded by Santo Trafficante Sr., who established strong ties to Cuba and died of natural causes in 1954. Trafficante Jr. (1914–1987), shown in the photo while entering the Kew Gardens Criminal Court in Queens in September 1966, took the place of his father, who had been overseeing his training for many years. The new godfather did business with the Bonanno family in New York City but had even stronger ties to Sam Giancana in Chicago. There are rumors he was in touch with the CIA concerning a plan to eliminate Fidel Castro, as well as secrets related to Jack Ruby, Lee Harvey Oswald, and the assassination of JFK. Able to avoid conviction and prison despite his position and the businesses he was involved in, he died from heart disease at the age of seventy-two.

37. The year is 1966, and the two men trying to hide their faces from the flashbulbs of photographers are Silvestro Carollo and Carlos Marcello, respectively the boss of the New Orleans family and his lieutenant. Carollo, nicknamed "Silver Dollar Sam," was born in Palermo in 1896 and created the family on the basis laid by the ancient Mano Nera. When Fiorello La Guardia became mayor of New York and banished gambling, confiscating and destroying every slot machine, Frank Costello did not lose heart and thought of his friend Carollo, moving his business to New Orleans. Deported to Italy after the Second World War, Carollo stayed put for twenty years, leaving control of the family to Carlos Marcello (1910–1993). Carollo returned to the United States in 1970 and died two years later.

38. The death of Jimmy Hoffa is still a mystery. Born into a poor family of German origins in Brazil, Indiana, on February 14, 1913, Hoffa became the powerful leader of the Teamsters union in the fifties and sixties. In 1964 he was sentenced to eight years in prison for corruption, a sentence he appealed for three years, going to prison in 1967. Released in December of 1971 with the obligation not to return to his union activity, Hoffa immediately sought to oppose the provision, but he met hostility from his own former colleagues. On July 30, 1975, he disappeared forever, perhaps after a meeting in a restaurant in the suburbs of Detroit with several members of the Mafia from Union City and New York. Declared legally dead in 1982, he was likely eliminated by the Cosa Nostra, in the conviction that his return to the top of the union could interfere with the interests of the criminal organization.

39. Stefano Magaddino was born in 1891 at Castellammare del Golfo, the birthplace of Joe Bonanno and many other members of the Costa Nostra. As early as 1921 he had been arrested for the murder of a man from a rival clan. He took part in the Castellamm-arese war, then moved to Niagara Falls, founding the Buffalo family. His stature earned him a seat on the Commission formed by Lucky Luciano in 1931 and he went on to become the boss with the longest record ruling a family, remaining in command for about fifty years, during which, it must be said, he escaped many attempts on his life. He died of a heart attack on July 19, 1974. He was succeeded by Samuel Frangiamore, known as "Sam the Farmer."

40. So died Angelo Bruno, on March 22, 1980, in Philadelphia, shot by a hit man. He had been born seventy years earlier, in Villalba, and had been nicknamed the "Gentle Don." Associated with the Gambino clan, he succeeded Joseph Ida in 1959 in command of the Philadelphia family. His leadership was sharply opposed, even internally, resulting in the murder, which was said to have been ordered by his consigliere Antonio Caponigro, known as "Tony Bananas." The consigliere's ambitious initiative had not been authorized by the other families, and a few weeks later Caponigro's body was found in the trunk of a car abandoned in New York, with $300 in bills stuffed into his mouth.

8 Corruption, Connivance, and Massacres

From the Sack of Palermo to the Second Mafia War

Construction contracts were a constant of Mafia gangs. So it had always been, but the so-called Sack of Palermo, the unprecedented construction boom based on building speculation, represents the high point of criminal control, supported by the alarming and open complicity of the business and political worlds. During the sixties and seventies, nearly every worksite in Palermo was controlled by the Cosa Nostra, and with it an incredible flow of money, so much that it seemed impossible to find an equally remunerative business.

Around 1975, however, the Mafia discovered another sector of investment capable of guaranteeing even greater earnings: heroin. Until then, the drug traffic had followed a route leading from the Middle East to Marseille. In that Provençal city the morphine base extracted from poppies was refined in laboratories controlled by the Corsican underworld, and from there it was distributed on the international market. The system was efficient and remained so until the French government began implementing policies to end it.

With an admirable sense of timing, the Sicilian Mafia stepped forward to take over the business, and in the span of a few months Palermo had been transformed into the world center for the refining of the drug. Thanks to contacts with the New York families, Gaetano Badalamenti and Salvatore Greco took over the international drug market, eventually controlling up to 90 percent of the U.S. market. From 1975 to 1984 the volume of business related to heroin exceeded $1.5 billion.

The Cosa Nostra did not limit itself to the production and shipment of the product but also worked to develop efficient distribution methods, hiding the merchandise in food products being shipped to hundreds of pizzerias spread over the United States.

Only when some traffickers were stopped at the Palermo airport was the size of the operation understood. The investigation, called the Pizza Connection and carried out with the collaboration of the FBI and the Italian police, led to the dismantling of the network and the bringing to justice of thirty-two mafiosi. But before the trial could take place the Second Mafia War broke out in Italy, a conflict so ferocious it has passed into Italian history as the *mattanza*—the "killing."

On one side were the Corleonesi of Riina and Provenzano, supported by the Ciaculli boss Michele Greco; on the other side was the faction composed of Tano Badalamenti, Stefano Bontate, Salvatore "Totuccio" Inzerillo, Tommaso Buscetta, Giuseppe Di Cristina, and Pippo Calderone.

The first to fall, signaling the beginning of the feud, was Giuseppe Di Cristina, the boss of Riesi, a town not far from Caltanissetta. Son and grandson of mafiosi, he was called the "Tiger" because of his ferocity. He was killed in Palermo on May 30, 1978.

Riina's next step was that of making an alliance with Nitto Santapaola, underboss to Pippo Calderone. Head of the families of Catania and secretary of the Commission, Calderone was a character from another time, a man of honor always eager to follow the route of mediation and avoid conflict. On September 9, 1978, Santapaola tricked him into going to Aci Castello, where one of his hit men mortally wounded him. From then on the escalation was unstoppable.

In 1978 Badalamenti was expelled from the Commission and escaped to America, and three years later Buscetta was forced to go into hiding in Brazil to flee killers who had massacred his family.

Between 1979 and 1980 perhaps as many as one thousand Corleone adversaries were killed. On April 23, 1981, Stefano Bontate was killed; on May 11 it was Salvatore Inzerillo. Carrying out this massacre was a real-life death squad, a group of murderers among whom stood out Leoluca Bagarella and Pino Greco, called *Scarpuzzedda* ("Little Shoe"). The two were responsible for more than 150 murders, guaranteeing Riina victory and the conquest of absolute hegemony over the Sicilian Cosa Nostra. The Corleonesi did not limit themselves to murdering the members of rival gangs, and their use of violence was systematic, directed at any person who obstructed them, whether investigators, judges, administrators, or honest politicians.

In March 1979 Michele Reina, provincial secretary of the Democratic Christian Party, was killed; on July 11 it was the Milanese lawyer Giorgio Ambrosoli; on July 21 the police chief Boris Giuliano was killed; on September 25 the judge Cesare Terranova. On January 6, 1980, it was the president of the Sicilian Region Piersanti Mattarella, followed by Emanuele Basile, a captain of the *carabinieri*.

The fearsome list continued with Gaetano Costa, Palermo's chief prosecutor; Vito Lipari, mayor of Castelvetrano; Pio La Torre, secretary of the Communist Party in Sicily and member of parliament; Carlo Alberto Dalla Chiesa, with his wife and bodyguard; Giangiacomo Ciaccio Montalto, assistant prosecutor of Trapani; the chief examining magistrate Rocco Chinnici; police inspectors Beppe Montana and Antonino (Ninni) Cassarà; the businessman Piero Patti; Giuseppe Insalaco, former mayor of Palermo; and the judge Antonino Saetta.

Even reporting Mafia corruption and trafficking earned a death warrant, so to the list of victims were added the names Peppino Impastato, Mario Francese, and Giuseppe Fava.

Yet the eighties were also the years of the Falcone and Borsellino investigations, the period that led the Anti-Mafia Pool to collect the documentation on Cosa Nostra crimes that eventually resulted in the Maxi trial of 1986.

1. Palermo was a beautiful city. A beautiful city, that is, before the "sack," the mindless construction speculation without precedent in Italian history. From the fifties to the mid-eighties the rule was first tear down, cancel forever an inestimable artistic patrimony, then heap up concrete, build immense apartment blocks one atop the next where previously had stood beautiful art nouveau villas with parks and gardens.

The saddest moment of the sack came during the period when Salvo Lima was mayor of the city and Vito Ciancimino was commissioner for public works. Both of them Christian Democrats, they were known for their ties to the Mafia, to the La Barberas, the Buscettas, but even more to the Corleonese family.

Over a period of a few years, forty-two hundred building permits were issued, of which more than three thousand were thought to be fraudulent, registered to fronts. Hundreds of building permits were given out in a single night in a perverse and perfect marriage between political corruption and Mafia business practices.

3. Pietro Scaglione (1906–1971) met his death at the exit from the cemetery where he had gone to pay his daily visit to his wife's grave. He got into the black Fiat 1300 together with his driver, Antonino Lo Russo, and the killers started shooting. The murder of the chief prosecutor of Palermo was the first "excellent cadaver" in Sicily since the days of Emanuele Notarbartolo, and although it was apparently carried out by Totò Riina, Luciano Liggio was behind the crime. Scaglione had been responsible for a legal measure that Liggio considered impolite. Not being able to send Liggio into confinement, because in fact Liggio was a fugitive in hiding, the prosecutor had arranged to apply the measure to one of the boss's sisters, a woman who had never been away from Corleone.

2. Mauro De Mauro was born in Foggia on September 6, 1921, and as a youth he enrolled in the Decima Mas of Junio Valerio Borghese. He had a brother, Tullio, who one day would be minister of education. He, instead, always curious about current events, decided to become a journalist and in 1959 was taken on by *L'Ora*, of Palermo, the most troublemaking daily paper in the city, the one least willing to shut an eye to gangsterism. That evening of September 16, 1970, having left the offices, he stopped in a bar to get himself coffee and cigarettes. He was approached by three men with whom he began to talk. He then became the victim of a lupara bianca, for nothing more was ever seen of him. That month he had again been investigating the mysterious death of Enrico Mattei, president of ENI, Italy's state-owned oil and gas conglomerate. De Mauro seems to have come into knowledge of uncomfortable truths. Or, according to the declaration of a *pentito*, the journalist was eliminated because he knew about the imminent right-wing coup d'état known as the Golpe Borghese.

4. Michele Greco, shown here in a youthful photo at the Circolo della Caccia of Palermo, was born in Ciaculli on May 12, 1924. His father, Giuseppe, called *Piddu 'u Tinenti* ("Piddu the Lieutenant"), was the boss of the Croce Verde–Giardini district, a position he handed on to his son. Michele was a decisive man but also able to mediate when necessary, for which reason he was nicknamed the "Pope." During the sixties and seventies he took to frequenting the leading society drawing rooms of Palermo. He himself welcomed politicians and businessmen into this splendid country estate at Ciaculli, and "friends" in difficulty with the law would be welcome there, as well as those needing assistance out of range of indiscreet eyes and ears.

After Gaetano Badalamenti was driven out of the Commission of the Cosa Nostra, the Pope was named to the Commission, a role he performed with the benevolent understanding of the Corleonese clan.

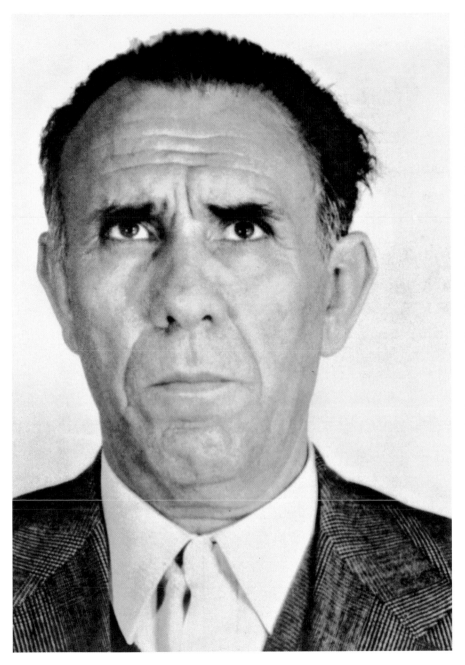

5. Gaetano Badalamenti, Don Tano, was born September 14, 1923, in Cinisi, of which he became the capo-mandamento. Charged with murder, in 1947 he fled to the United States but was deported three years later. After a period of relative silence, following the Ciaculli massacre and the First Mafia War, in 1970 the Mafia Commission was revived, this time directed by a triumvirate composed of Badalamenti, Stefano Bontate, and Luciano Liggio. At the end of the seventies Don Tano ruled the traffic in heroin imported from the Middle East, refined in Sicily, and sold on the American market. The Corleonesi's growing influence on the Commission led to him being driven out, replaced by Michele Greco. The FBI also took aim at him, asking for his extradition in 1984. The next year the so-called Pizza Connection trial began in Manhattan, destined to last nearly two years. It ended with Badalamenti being given a prison sentence of forty-five years for drug trafficking, money laundering, and criminal conspiracy. During his incarceration he never showed the slightest willingness to disassociate himself from the Mafia or to repent, and in fact he refused to corroborate Tommaso Buscetta's testimony, which implicated him many times.

In 2002 Badalamenti was sentenced to life in prison for ordering the murder of Peppino Impastato, which occurred on May 9, 1978. On April 29, 2004, at the age of eighty-one, Gaetano Badalamenti died from cardiac arrest at the Federal Medical Center in Devens, Massachusetts.

6–7. In the beginning there was the forced exile of those who had fallen out of favor with those in power, obliging such people to live far from home. Forcing people who displeased the government to relocate, obliging them to live far from their homes, was originally called *domicilio coatto* ("forced residence"). During the period of fascism this forced residence was called *confino di polizia* and had more to do with politics than with the law. Finally, in 1956, a law of the republic defined it *soggiorno obbligato*. In May 1971, fifteen leading members of the Mafia were victims of this measure. They belonged to the Greco and Corleonese clans and were sent to Filicudi (one of the Lipari Islands), while another seventeen, affiliated with the La Barbera clan, were sent to Linosa (one of the Pelagie Islands).

The photos on these pages present moments in the lives of the mafiosi sent to Linosa. Among those visible in the photo below are Rosario Riccobono (far left), the boss of Partana Mondello; Riccobono was said to be in possession of one of the most famous works of art ever stolen, the *Nativity with Saints Lawrence and Francis of Assisi* by Caravaggio, taken from the Oratorio of San Lorenzo in Palermo in October 1969. Riccobono was killed in November of 1982, according to several *pentiti*, garroted by Pino Greco.

8. In the summer of 1971 a photographer surprised a pretty girl with a smile on her face walking down the hallway of Palermo's courthouse. This was Antonietta Bagarella, and she was twenty-seven and a schoolteacher. Ninetta, as she was known to everyone, was born in Corleone and grew up in a family in which the code of the Mafia was well known. Her father ended up with a *soggiorno obbligato*; Calogero and Leoluca Bagarella were her brothers. As if this weren't enough, Ninetta fell in love with Calogero's best friend, Salvatore Riina, known as "Totò," and they became engaged.

That is how she came to be walking along the hall of Palermo's courthouse. She was convicted of aiding and abetting, but the charge was dropped in the appeals court. Ninetta married Totò Riina on April 16, 1974, and stayed beside him during his life on the run, giving him four children.

9. The Trial of the 114, named for the number of the defendants, began in July 1974 in a court in Catanzaro, on the Italian mainland, held there because of larger facilities but also in the hope of protecting the witnesses and getting a fair trial.

The crime of Mafia association did not yet exist, so there was only the crime of criminal association; thus people like the Rimi brothers and Pippo Calò got away without great damage. It was less easy for Angelo La Barbera, Pietro Torretta, and "the boss of two worlds," as Tommaso Buscetta (in the photo above on left) was called because of his activity on both sides of the Atlantic. Born in Palermo in 1928, Buscetta (also known as Don Masino) joined the Porta Nuova crime family when still a boy. At the end of the Second World War he tried his fortune first in Argentina, then in Brazil, and around 1950 he returned to Sicily, joining the La Barbera clan.

During the early sixties he built an empire in South America founded on the drug traffic. Arrested in Brazil in 1972, he was extradited to Italy. While on day release he managed to escape and fled back to Brazil, but during the Second Mafia War he saw his family exterminated by the Corleonsi. Arrested and sent back to Italy, he attempted suicide before asking to talk to Giovanni Falcone.

10. Giuseppe Russo (1926–1977), a colonel in the *carabinieri*, was one of the most capable investigators in Palermo; too capable, in the opinion of Totò Riina and Bernardo Provenzano, who sent a crew of hit men out for him, among them Leoluca Bagarella and Pino Greco. On August 20, 1977, in Ficuzza, a fraction of Corleone, Russo decided to go for a walk with his friend Filippo Costa, a professor whose work had nothing to do with that of the colonel. Neither of the men noticed the Fiat 128 that followed them and went past only to turn and stop a short distance away. What followed was a cruel execution using pistols and rifles and coups de grâce in the heads of both victims. On October 29, 1997, twenty years after the double murder, the appeals court of Palermo sentenced Bagarella, Riina, and Provenzano to life imprisonment.

11. The man on the right, in hand-cuffs with his shirt open, is Gaspare Mutolo, born in Palermo in 1940. He seems to have been a common thief until he met Totò Riina in prison. He then began his career as a Mafia criminal with special skills in the international traffic of heroin. Today he has turned state's evidence and paints pictures.

The man on the far left is a hero of our time. This is the police chief Boris Giuliano (1930–1979). Gifted with sharp instincts as an investigator, he was getting ready to deliver a hard blow to the drug market and reveal the involvement of political and financial interests when the Mafia decreed his death.

On the morning of July 21, 1979, Giuliano went to a bar in Via de Blasi, Palermo, to get a coffee. Leoluca Bagarella came in behind him and shot him seven times with a pistol.

"I thought a 'hero' had to be a solemn person, always serious and also a little sad. That is the opposite of my father, a simple man, easy to be around and so happy! After years I understood that my father truly was a hero." These are the words of Alessandro, Boris's son, who is following in his footsteps and today directs the flying squad of Milan.

12. Giuseppe "Peppino" Impastato had the courage to rebel. He became a political activist and joined peasants and workers in their protests, founded a radio station that denounced Mafia trafficking, and organized protests against organized crime. What made such a big difference was that his affirmations were not generic statements but always direct accusations with first and last names. Gaetano Badalamenti, in particular, was a target of his attacks.

Born at Cinisi, in the province of Palermo, on January 5, 1948, Peppino was the son of a Mafia family, with a father sent into exile during the fascist period, and he was related to the boss Cesare Manzella. But rather than follow the rules of the Cosa Nostra, he preferred to end the relationship and leave home. On May 9, 1978, a powerful charge of TNT put an end to his life. Only a few months earlier he had celebrated his thirtieth birthday.

13–14. "The motive for the Francese crime arises from his professional activity, in the extraordinary dedication to public service with which he assembled an in-depth reconstruction of the most complex and important Mafia events of the seventies." So wrote the judges that sentenced Leoluca Bagarella and Nino Madonia as the material executors of the murder and Riina, Provenzano, and Michele Greco as those who had ordered it. Mario Francese (1925–1979) was the first to discern the power and ferocity with which the Corleonese clan was preparing to take over the Cosa Nostra, from the Ciaculli massacre on. And when Colonel Russo was killed, Francese wanted to lay it bare and understand which interests the investigator had uncovered. Just before being killed he published an article in his newspaper, *Il Giornale di Sicilia*, with an emblematic title and explosive contents: "The Republic of the Mafiosi." That evening, January 26, 1979, Francese left the editorial offices of his paper late. He was intercepted near his home and was given no chance to escape.

15–16. Opposite is Roberto Calvi in a hall of the Milan court in 1981; to the right above is his cadaver just after been taken off the Blackfriars Bridge in London, where he was killed in a faked suicide. Calvi (1920–1982) began his career in Italy's Banco Ambrosiano at the end of the forties, becoming its general director and finally chairman. His close association with ecclesiastical circles earned him the nickname "God's Banker," while his friendship with Michele Sindona, which began in 1968, was at first a business relationship and then an open conflict. His death began an inquest that ended with indictments of Giuseppe "Pippo" Calò, known as the "Mafia's cashier," the unscrupulous businessman Flavio Carboni, and Ernesto Diotallevi, one of the leaders of the Banda Magliana, a criminal organization based in Rome. The hypothesis that Calvi was killed because he had administered the Mafia's money poorly seemed quite possible, but then in June 2007 the criminal court in Rome absolved those charged on the basis of insufficient evidence. The murder of Roberto Calvi and the dense web between Mafia, finance, politics, and freemasonry has yet to be fully untangled.

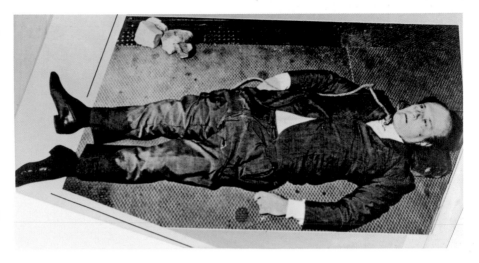

17. In 1974, to clarify the state of the credit institutions directed by Michele Sindona, the court appointed a liquidator, choosing the forty-one-year-old Milanese lawyer Giorgio Ambrosoli. Honest and highly competent, Ambrosoli immediately became aware of serious irregularities, of manipulations between declared activities and uncertain operations with obscure purposes.

As he examined files and documents he began receiving suggestions that, week by week, became less and less friendly, to the point that after a year of work, in a letter to his wife, Ambrosoli wrote, "Without a doubt, whatever happens, I will pay a high price for this job: I knew it before accepting it, so I am not complaining because it has been a unique opportunity for me to do something for my country."

The date set for the conclusion of the inquest and the presentation of the final report was July 12, 1979. The evening of the day before, while returning home, Giorgio Ambrosoli was shot three times in the heart by William Joseph Aricò, a killer in the pay of Michele Sindona, who was sentenced to life imprisonment in March 1986 for the crime.

18–19. Michele Sindona was born at Patti, Sicily, in May 1920. During the postwar years enterprise and unscrupulousness made it possible for him to accumulate large sums of money and to take control of several banks, both in Italy and elsewhere. Without doubt associated with freemasonry and political spheres, he has long been spoken of in relation to the IOR—the Instituto per le Opere di Religione ("Institute for Works of Religion")—of Cardinal Paul Marcinkus, a circumstance always sharply denied by the Vatican.

The boldness that made him a magician of international finance also, however, decreed his downfall, with the failure of the Franklin National Bank in 1974. Sindona's financial problems were also a problem for the Cosa Nostra, given that, according to the Mafia *pentito* Francesco Marino Mannoia, the banker's roles had included that of laundering money from the drug traffic of the Bontate-Spatola-Inzerillo-Gambino ring. Convicted on sixty-five counts in the United States in 1980 (where the Italian journalist Enzo Biagi, to the right in the photo, met him for an interview), he was extradited to Italy to face trial for the death of Ambrosoli.

On March 29, 1986, in a cell of the prison of Voghera, someone added cyanide to Sindona's cup of coffee. He died after two days of agony. Even today it is difficult to understand what happened. The poison has an odor too pungent for him not to have noticed its presence, making it seem possible that Sindona took it voluntarily. Not to kill himself, however, but to make himself ill and convince officials that detention in Italy was too dangerous, so as to return him to the United States. But perhaps his accomplice, charged with doctoring his beverage, "made a mistake" in the dosage.

20. First, in 1969, he tried to prosecute Luciano Liggio and more than sixty Corleonesi in Bari, but he failed to obtain the results he hoped for. He tried again in 1974, and this time Liggio was given life imprisonment.

Cesare Terranova (1921–1979) had reason to be satisfied, but his dedication drove him to try more and led him into politics, serving as a representative in the Italian parliament from 1976 to 1979. He then returned to the judiciary, becoming chief examining magistrate for Palermo. On September 25, 1979, as on every morning, the escort car arrived to take him to work. The judge sat in the driver's seat next to the officer, Lenin Mancuso, who had been beside him for twenty years. Following a secondary route, the two suddenly found a barrier blocking their way. They reacted immediately but not fast enough to stop the killers. In January 2000 the criminal court of Reggio Calabria gave life sentences to Salvatore Riina, Bernardo Brusca, Bernardo Provenzano, Francesco Madonia, Pippo Calò, Antonio Geraci, and Michele Greco, all of them accused of ordering the double homicide.

21. Surrounded by *carabinieri* as he was, and even with handcuffs on his wrists, Leoluca Bagarella seemed to burst with rage when he was arrested in December 1979. The person who ended up getting hurt was the photographer, Letizia Battaglia, kicked while taking the picture. The pain was more than repaid by the photo's terrible realism.

Leoluca, son of Salvatore and brother of Calogero and Ninetta, was not just anyone; a ruthless killer, born in Palermo in 1942, he climbed the hierarchy of the Corleone family until he and Provenzano occupied the summit of the family following the arrests of Liggio and then Riina.

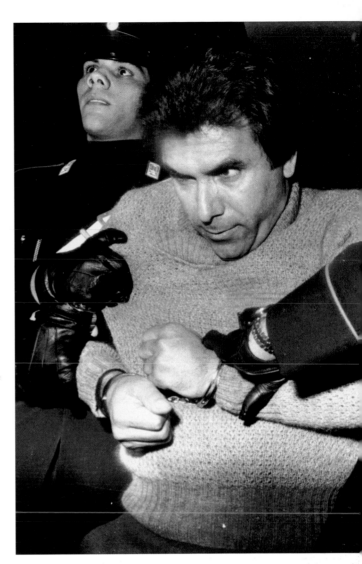

22. A family of Christian Democrats, that of the Mattarella, with the father, Bernardo, a politician who was the minister of Italy several times, and his two sons, Sergio and Piersanti. Piersanti, born in Castellammare del Golfo in 1935, followed the most noble ideals of the DC (Democrazia Cristiana, Christian Democrats), inspired by the politics of Giorgio La Pira and in turn wanted to put himself in the service of others.

Deputy to the regional parliament of Sicily in 1967, he became president in 1978 at the head of a center left coalition supported by the Communist Party of Pio La Torre. In this position he proposed introducing transparency in investments and in the direction of agricultural contributions. This was too threatening to the Mafia, which sent a gunman to kill him while he was in his car alongside his wife and son, on January 6, 1980.

23. He was the first to go, Stefano Bontate, he who loved to be called the "Prince of Villagrazia" (from the name of the section of Palermo he controlled and his home on Via Villagrazia) and was the son of Don Paolino, the boss photographed at the funeral of Don Calogero Vizzini (page 109). On April 23, 1981, he was driving home from his forty-second birthday party when two hit men killed him with shots from a Kalashnikov. It was a sign that times were changing, that someone was no longer willing to let the Bontate, Inzerillo, and Badalamenti families run things. That someone was the Corleonesi, and their intention was to wipe out their rivals.

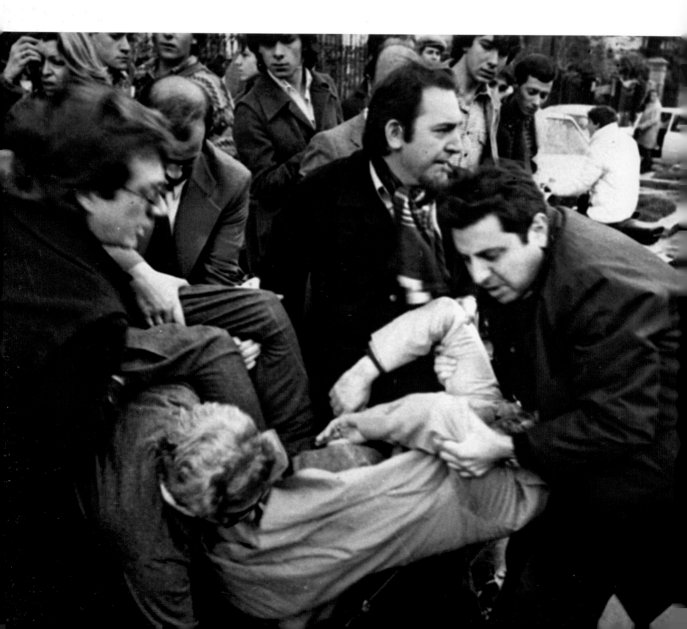

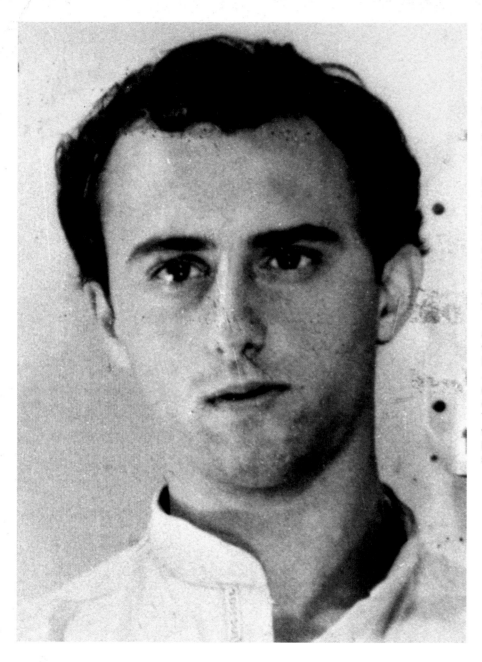

24–25. After Bontate came Salvatore Inzerillo (1944–1981), called Totuccio and the boss of the Passo di Rigano family; faithful ally of Badalamenti and Bontate, he boasted a cousin of the caliber of Carlo Gambino, which opened the way for him to become one of the leading heroin traffickers of the seventies.

On May 11, 1981, he visited his girlfriend, with whom he spent a few hours. On his way out he didn't even have time to reach his bulletproof Alfetta, which could have protected him from the shots. The forensic doctor examining his body (opposite) could do little but confirm his death and arrange for the body to be taken to the morgue.

Behind the murders of Bontate and Inzerillo, killed only a few weeks apart, was the same hit man, Pino Greco, called *Scarpuzzedda* ("Little Shoe"). But even he met an ugly end, victim of a *lupara bianca* on the orders of Totò Riina, whom he had probably wronged a few times but primarily because he had begun to show signs of unhealthy ambition.

26–27. The story of Pio La Torre (1927–1982) is somewhat similar to that of Piersanti Mattarella; although belonging to different political groups, both men spent their lives working for the public good, and both met a tragic death at the hands of criminals protecting their own interests.

La Torre's career began with the unions, CGIL, and continued in the Italian Communist Party. He became a member of parliament in 1972 and proposed the idea for a law that would introduce the crime of membership in a Mafia-type association, including the right of the courts to seize and confiscate illegally acquired property (the law, known as the Rognoni–La Torre Anti-Mafia Law,

was approved ten years later, in 1982). Regional secretary of the Communist Party in Sicily in 1981, he opposed the construction of the Comiso Air Base and began a battle against construction speculation.

On the morning of April 30, 1982, while driving to the Communist Party headquarters with his colleague Rosario Di Salvo, large motorcycles pulled up alongside the car. The two friends died under the bullets of the killers. According to a mafioso who turned state's evidence, the instigator of the murder, initially claimed by the left-wing Gruppi Proletari Organizzati, had been Totò Riina, worried about La Torre's determination to attack mafiosi by going after their assets.

28–29. The photo above shows Ninni Cassarà, Giovanni Falcone, and Rosso Chinnici at the scene of the murder of Pio La Torre. The image, printed by local daily papers on the day after the crime, was cut out and sent to Judge Falcone several months later as a warning, a very clear threat since meanwhile the Mafia had killed both police inspector Cassarà and the judge Chinnici. Rocco Chinnici (1925–1983) entered the judiciary in 1952, holding several posts before being nominated investigating magistrate. His work and that of Antonino Caponnetto, who succeeded him, laid the groundwork for the Maxi trial of 1986. On July 29, 1983, a Fiat stuffed with TNT was blown up by remote control by Pino Greco. Aside from the many wounded, four people died in this slaughter on Via Pipitone Federico (opposite): Chinnici; two of his bodyguards, Mario Trapassi and Salvatore Bartolotta; and the concierge of his apartment house, Stefano Li Sacchi.

30–31–32. The life story of Carlo Alberto Dalla Chiesa (1920–1982) is deeply interwoven with that of modern Sicily. He was born to his role, his father having been a *carabiniere* under the prefect Cesare Mori; he joined the military in 1942 and in 1943 fought among the ranks of the partisans.

At the end of the war his first posting was the headquarters of Casoria, near Naples, then he was a member of the group under Colonel Ugo Luca active in the repression of banditry. In 1948 he investigated the murder of Placido Rizzotto before being given assignments in Rome and Milan. From 1966 to 1973 he was in Sicily again, investigating the most outrageous Mafia attacks, from the slaughter in Viale Lazio to the murder of Judge Scaglione, and helping prepare the cases for the Trial of the 114. In 1974, as brigadier general, he created a special antiterrorism squad, dedicating himself to fighting the Red Brigades. In 1982, with his impressive experience and in the wake of the successes he had obtained in the struggle against the Red Brigades, he was named prefect of Palermo. He made his official arrival in the city in May and

immediately realized that the support being provided to him by the state was insufficient. He complained, protesting the lack of personnel, the distance of the authorities. Despite this, his work as an investigator began to achieve important results.

All of this ended on September 3, shortly after midnight, in Palermo's Via Isidoro Carini. A BMW pulled alongside the car in which he was riding with his wife, Emanuela, and machine-gun blasts killed both of them while behind them another hit man killed their bodyguard, Domenico Russo. The next day, a sign appeared on the site of the crime on which was written, "Here dies the hope of every honest citizen of Palermo."

Emanuela Setti Carraro had become Dalla Chiesa's wife only two months before dying with him. A nurse, she had fallen in love with the general and had convinced him to marry despite the difference in their ages. She had been the only person always beside him during the weeks that preceded the murder. Inside the bullet-ridden car Dalla Chiesa was found hugging his wife in a futile effort to protect her from the killers' bullets.

33. The question of the relationship between Giulio Andreotti (born 1919) and the Mafia is complex, with overlapping testimonies and inferences, operations designed to discredit or to rehabilitate. Investigated for his hypothetical complicity in Mafia association, he was acquitted in 1999, and in 2003 he was acquitted of ties to the Mafia but with a distinction made between events that happened before and after 1980. For the earlier years he was culpable of criminal association, but that was annulled for reason of expiry of statutory terms. For the later years the senator for life was absolved. The appeals court repeated these conclusions in 2004. The outcome of the trial would probably have been different had the final sentence been reached before December 2002, the last date for time allowed.

34. Salvatore Achille Ettore Lima, known as Salvo Lima, was born in Palermo on January 23, 1928, and died there sixty-four years later, the victim of pistol shots fired by Mafia hit men. Vice mayor of Palermo from 1956 to 1958, then mayor from 1959 to 1963 and again from 1965 to 1968, he was the leader of the Christian Democratic Party in Sicily for years in the political faction associated with Giulio Andreotti.

35. The political career of Vito Alfio Ciancimino (1924–2002) coincides with the years of the Sack of Palermo, when he was the commissioner for public works under Mayor Salvo Lima. He himself was mayor, although for only a few months, between 1970 and 1971. Around 1980 word got out about collusion between Ciancimino, Lima, and the Corleonese family. These rumors were repeated and confirmed by Tommaso Buscetta in the declarations he gave judges. The photo shows the moment of Ciancimino's arrest, in 1984. In 1993 he was convicted of Mafia association.

36. Giangiacomo Ciaccio Montalto (1941–1983) was hardly more than forty years old when the Mafia had him killed on the evening of January 25, 1983, as he made his way home to his wife and three daughters. With his institutional memory of the Trapani prosecutor's office, where he had worked since 1971, he made an unwelcome figure to the Trapanesi gangs and to the Minore family. He had no hesitation about applying the recently passed Rognoni–La Torre law, for which reason he received clear threats. A few weeks more and his requested transfer to Tuscany would have come through.

37–38. Leonardo Vitale was remembered only after Tommaso Buscetta began collaborating with the law. In fact Vitale was the first Mafia *pentito*, although no one has ever given him credit. After months passed reflecting sadly on his career as a man of honor, Leonardo—Leuccio to his friends—decided he'd had enough and one day in March 1973 presented himself to the Palermo police station and tried to tell the officers everything he knew about Riina and Provenzano, Greco and Ciancimino. The officers did not even take the trouble to check his statement. They claimed his confessions were the ravings of a mad man and sent him away to spend ten years in the mental asylum for criminals in the town of Barcellona Pozzo di Gotto in Sicily. This did nothing to diminish his repentance, which was the fruit of a spiritual crisis. Finally released from the asylum, he used his Fiat 500 to go to Mass every morning in the Church of the Cappuccini. Two months after his release, on December 2, 1984, the Mafia showed Leonardo and Italy that it never forgets traitors.

39. Judges, investigators, and journalists were not the only ones to fall victim to the Mafia. There were also honest businessmen, people who did not want to give in to the blackmail of the Cosa Nostra. People like Roberto Parisi, killed with his driver Giuseppe Mangano on February 23, 1985, because he "would not cooperate," or like Piero Patti, who fell victim to the Mafia only five days later.

Patti was killed in his car; his daughter Gaia, whom he was taking to school, was wounded. The businessman had been guilty of refusing to give in to extortion.

40. Giuseppe "Pippo" Fava (1925–1984), shown opposite, was a figure outside the ordinary: journalist, writer for theater and film, director of the *Giornale del Sud*, founder and editor of the magazine *I Siciliani*. And always, no matter what, on the front line in denouncing the crimes of the Mafia. A week before being killed, in an interview with Enzo Biagi, he declared, "I realize there's an enormous amount of confusion concerning the problem of the Mafia. Mafiosi are in Parliament, mafiosi are sometimes ministers, mafiosi are bankers, mafiosi are those who at this very moment are the leaders of this nation."

Five 7.65-caliber bullets stopped him on January 5, 1985. The first hypothesis spoke of a crime of passion, then of a matter of money and debts. The truth was obviously something else, and in 1998 the Catania boss Nitto Santapaola was sentenced to life in prison for ordering the crime.

41. The photo shows police inspector Giuseppe "Beppe" Montana in the dark jacket at right with his men at the conclusion of an operation in which they uncovered an arsenal of Mafia weapons. Montana was then young, born in Agrigento in 1951, but he was one of the most capable inspectors active on Palermo's flying squad and had worked with Judge Chinnici. The gunmen waited for him at Porticello, where he had moored his small boat and was taking a walk with his girlfriend. This was on July 28, 1985; nine days later it was his colleague Ninni Cassarà who fell victim to murderers.

9 The Buscetta Theorem

The Season of the Maxi Trial

"We entered the council chamber on November 10, 1987, and stayed there thirty-five days, completely isolated from the world . . . it was undoubtedly the longest deliberation in chambers in the memory of man. Our typical day (we were two gowned judges and six jurors) began at nine in the morning with a break at one for lunch, and began again at three in the afternoon until eight at night, when it was time for dinner."

These are the words of Pietro Grasso, today chief prosecutor of the national anti-Mafia bureau, at the time a judge in the Maxi trial of Palermo.

The Maxi trial, the first formidable blow delivered to the Mafia, began on February 10, 1986, in the special bunker built in record time alongside Palermo's Ucciardone prison. But the work required to arrive at the first hearing had begun many years earlier, between the end of 1979 and the beginning of 1980.

After the murder of Judge Cesare Terranova, Rocco Chinnici took his place as Palermo's chief prosecutor; he entrusted one of the many briefs to forty-year-old Giovanni Falcone. The brief related to the investigation of the powerful mafioso family in Palermo's Uditore residential district, and the judge proceeded with his special method, searching for ties and connections but most of all paying close attention to financial records, tracing the flow of money.

The investigation greatly troubled the Cosa Nostra, as well as the politicians, businessmen, and operators tied to the Mafia, and together they endeavored to block Falcone's work, their efforts destined to become a constant reality for Falcone's entire career.

A few weeks after sending a judiciary communication to Nino and Ignazio Salvo, Chinnici was killed in a dynamite attack. To take his place Antonino Caponnetto arrived in Palermo from Florence, and it was thanks to him that in November 1983 the Anti-Mafia Pool came into existence, composed of four men: Giovanni Falcone, Paolo Borsellino, Leonardo Guarnotta, and Giuseppe Di Lello.

Following three years of difficult work, its prosecutors obliged to confront a wall of omertà on facts as well as the coldness if not hostility of colleagues and institutions, the indictment that would eventually bring more than seven hundred mafiosi to justice began taking shape.

A decisive contribution to the structure of the indictment was provided by Tommaso Buscetta, who in July 1984, before Falcone and the director of Criminalpol Gianni De Gennaro, began to recount everything he knew about the Mafia. And the fifty-six-year-old Buscetta knew a good deal about the Cosa Nostra, including its structure, dynamics, behind-the-scenes dealings, and crimes.

An effective way to describe Buscetta's contribution is to see it as the Rosetta stone of the Mafia, a lexicon, a code with which to interpret the Mafia alphabet, long guessed at but never completely revealed.

Until then, the Cosa Nostra had been dismissed as a loose assembly of criminal gangs, but the thousands of pages of Buscetta's statement reveal its hierarchical structure, with a commission and leaders overseeing those who commit criminal acts. This view of the Mafia came to be called the Buscetta theorem.

Nor was Buscetta the only one to help the Anti-Mafia Pool, for there were also such extraordinary police inspectors as Ninni Cassarà and Beppe Montana, both of whom paid with their lives for their intelligence and courage. Fully twenty-two months were needed to reach the first verdicts, with nineteen life sentences and more than twenty-six hundred years of imprisonment.

This was a hard blow to the Mafia, and during the period of waiting for the outcome of the appeals process at all its levels, the efforts to delegitimize the Anti-Mafia Pool began, directed most of all against Giovanni Falcone, its leading figure. A first important moment came with the nomination of the successor to Caponnetto. In terms of competency, background, and most of all familiarity with the material there was no doubt that Falcone was the right judge for the position, but there was a surprise candidate, a judge on the eve of retirement who thus had a great deal of career seniority. His name was Antonio Meli, and he was the one chosen for the post. He soon distinguished himself for the diligence with which he attacked the investigations brought ahead by Falcone. Where the younger judge had sought to unify, grouping trials and crimes under a common denominator, Meli instead took each inquest and divided it up to distribute the various pieces to the applicable prosecutors according to the territories involved.

In response to this attack, which upset the Anti-Mafia Pool, Falcone wrote a letter to the Consliglio Superiore della Magistratura (CSM), the body that oversees Italy's judicial branch.

On July 30, 1988, in tones expressing his great disturbance, he wrote: "What I feared would happen has taken place: the investigations into the Mafia have bogged down, and that delicate mechanism known as the Anti-Mafia Pool of the investigative office of Palermo, for reasons that cannot be analyzed in this forum, has stalled."

Falcone was to suffer further disappointments, such as the nomination of Domenico Sica as the anti-Mafia high commissioner, a role that by all rights should have gone to him. He then had to endure the attempts at character assassination in anonymous defamatory letters that presented serious charges, most of all in regard to Salvatore "Totuccio" Contorno, a pentito taken away from Italy, who was arrested in Palermo in May of 1989. According to the letters Falcone, together with De Gennaro, had brought Contorno back with the aim of transforming him into a state killer of the Corleonesi enemies.

Then came the story of the Addaura bomb.

Falcone rented a beach house for the summer every year on the strip of coastline between Mondello and Palermo near the town of Addaura, and on June 20, 1989, fifty-eight sticks of dynamite and plastic explosives were found in a sports bag left on the rocks in front of the beach house. A slanderous rumor immediately spread through Palermo: that Falcone himself had put the bomb there and that is was all faked, anything but a real murder attempt. Today we have learned that behind the operation was not only the Mafia but deviated secret services of the state.

The Corleonesi went after not only the judges but also those among their "friends" who had imprudently guaranteed them that the appeals courts would undo the sentences of the Maxi trial. It was probably for that reason that Salvo Lima and Ignazio Salvo died.

1–2. The Second Mafia War became a bloodbath for the family of Tommaso Buscetta. He lost two sons and four nephews, a brother, a son-in-law, and a brother-in-law (the photo below shows the last-named victim).

He was arrested in Brazil in 1983, and in June 1984 São Paulo's supreme federal court gave its consent to his extradition. On his arrival in Italy Buscetta decided to collaborate with the judges, in particular Giovanni Falcone. He did not declare him- self a *pentito*, but he no longer felt he belonged in the Mafia of Riina and Provenzano. His testimony (opposite, during the Maxi trial of 1986) made it possible to recon- struct the structure and organiza- tion of the Cosa Nostra. Once again he was extradited, this time to the United States, where he was put in the Witness Protection Program under a new identity and given his freedom in exchange for further information. He died of a tumor in April 2000, at the age of seventy-two.

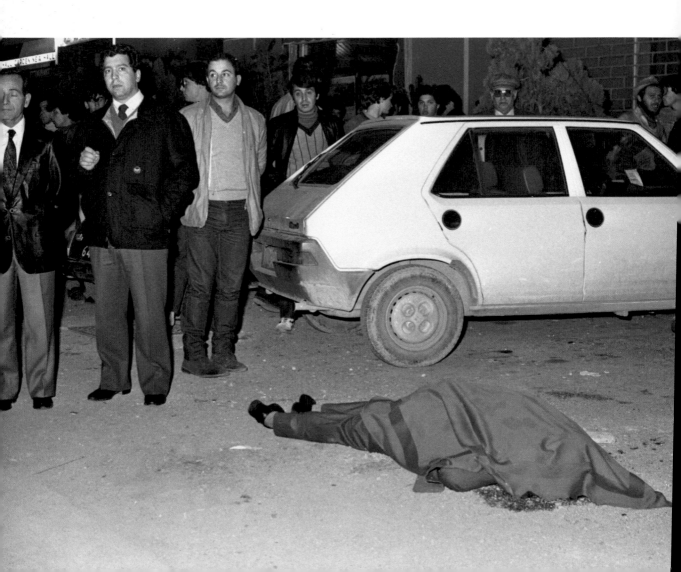

3–4. They were only cousins, but people spoke of the Di Salvos as though they were a single entity. Even in photos they had a lot in common, such as those of their arrests in 1984, that of Ignazio opposite, Nino's above.

Businessmen, politicians, mafiosi—the Di Salvos endeavored to exploit every opportunity to ally themselves with anyone in power and then to reap the benefits, just as they had no hesitation about abandoning allies in decline, such as the Bontate and Badalamenti families, in favor of reaching a more profitable understanding with the Corleonesi.

Both were born in Salemi, Sicily, Nino in 1929, Ignazio three years later. Their power came to them from possession of a monopoly on the collection of taxes in Sicily; there were no imposts that did not require a percentage pocketed by the "collectors," as they were called.

On November 12, 1984, Giovanni Falcone asked for their arrest for Mafia association; Nino died of a tumor in 1986, but Ignazio's death sentence was pronounced by Totò Riina and was carried out by a team of hit men led by Leoluca Bagarella, on September 17, 1992.

5–6. Head of the Mafia Commission after the expulsion of Tano Badalamenti, Michele "the Pope" Greco was arrested on February 20, 1986. The Maxi trial had just begun, making it possible to put him behind bars in the bunker courtroom in Palermo together with his many "friends." Although he sought to deny every involvement in criminal activity, claiming it was only a matter of misunderstandings or, at most, malice, the court sentenced him to six life sentences.

Before the judges and jurors retired to the deliberation chamber Greco asked to make a spontaneous declaration, in the style of the perfect mafioso: "Signor Judge, I would like to wish you peace . . . because peace is tranquillity of the spirit, the conscience. And for the duty that awaits you, serenity is the foundation on which to judge. Those aren't my words, they're the words of our lord who commanded Moses: 'When you must judge, decide with utmost serenity.' And I wish, Signor Judge, that this peace accompanies you for the rest of your life."

When his health deteriorated he was moved from the prison to a clinic, and he died on February 13, 2008.

Opposite, Mafia boss Luciano Liggio during a hearing in the Maxi trial.

7. In September 1979, two months after killing Boris Giuliano, Leoluca Bagarella (shown opposite in the bunker-courtroom in Palermo) was arrested and then sentenced. In 1986, on the eve of the Maxi trial, he was again captured on instructions from Judge Falcone, to serve a four-year prison term. A fugitive since 1992, with the arrest of Totò Riina he became the leading man in the Corleonese family, along with Bernardo Provenzano. On June 24, 1995, officers of the DIA (anti-Mafia investigation department) intercepted him in his car in Palermo. He tried to flee but covered only a few hundred yards before surrendering. He was found guilty of the cases held against him and was sentenced to life in prison for a number of murders, among them those of the police chief Giuliano and young Giuseppe di Matteo, as well as for the Capaci massacre.

8. Giuseppe Calò, known as "Pippo" (on the left in the photo below), was born in Palermo on September 30, 1931. At the end of the sixties he became the undisputed boss of the Porta Nuova Mafia family. A good nose for business led him to invest the Mafia's money in profitable operations, and he became known as the "Mafia's Cashier." In association with the Corleonesi, he had no hesitation about establishing working relationships with the world of finance while making an alliance with the Banda della Magliana. He was among those responsible for the slaughter on the Naples–Milan Express 904, in which seventeen people were killed on December 23, 1984. Calò was arrested on March 30, 1985. Aside from the train attack, he was sentenced to life in prison for his involvement in the murder of Boris Giuliano and the murder of Carlo Alberto Dalla Chiesa and his wife and bodyguard in Palermo's Via Carini.

9–10. Francesco Marino Mannoia (born 1951) has not earned a catchy nickname, like those that usually distinguish an important boss. In fact, he was usually called "Mozzarella" or the "Chemist" because of his skill in using alembics to refine the crude heroin that arrived from Marseille and was destined for the American market. He worked first for Stefano Bontate, then was forced to accept working for the Corleonesi. The murder of his younger brother convinced him to reconsider his situation. It was his mistress Rita, the person he loved and who had given him a daughter, who convinced him, and she herself went to the police to announce that Marino Mannoia wanted to give himself up and collaborate. Francesco Marino Mannoia was the first *pentito* after Leonardo Vitale, and his testimony provided important clues concerning the death of Calvi, the role of Sindona, about Licio Gelli and Pippo Calò and many others.

The revenge of the Cosa Nostra is fearsome and does not hesitate to strike women, and so it was that Marino Mannoia's mother was killed as were his sister and aunt (in the photo opposite). His knowledge of criminal acts related to the Cosa Nostra in the United States guaranteed him American citizenship and entry in the FBI's Witness Protection Program. No one knows the name Francesco Marino Mannoia goes by today, nor where he is.

9 The Buscetta Theorem

11–12. Rosario Livantino (above, standing in the middle) was born in Canicatti on October 3, 1952, the only son of Vincenzo, a lawyer, and Rosalia. He was a shy boy, serious but not overly active in the Azione Cattolica. In 1975 he earned a degree in jurisprudence at Palermo and in 1978, age twenty-six, he got a position as magistrate. Livantino was only thirty-eight when a group of four hit men killed him, on September 21, 1990, while on the state road 640, from Caltanissetta to Agrigento. He was killed because in Agrigento, where he worked, he had begun to investigate corruption, the Mafia in construction, subjects that would be part of the Sicilian *tangentopoli* ("bribes city") scandal. Pope John Paul II said of Livatino that he was "a martyr of justice and in an indirect way of the Christian faith." In 2010, twenty years after his death, the process began for his beatification.

13. The time came when Libero Grassi just couldn't put up with it anymore. He wasn't young, having been born in 1924, and he came from a family of proven antifascists. He'd been given the name Libero in memory of Giacomo Matteotti, the politician and defender of liberty who'd been killed by fascist thugs because of his honesty and values. Grassi could no longer accept being put upon by requests to pay the *pizzo* (protection money) on the earnings of his underwear factory in Sicily. And his workers were on his side. He published a letter in the *Giornale di Sicilia* in which he expressed all his anger and his desire to not give in to blackmail and extortion (the letter began, "Dear Extortionist"). He was interviewed on television and became an example even outside Italy's borders. But other businessmen did not follow his example, and even the institutions went no further than generic support and empty remarks.

On August 29, 1991, he was killed outside his home. After that he was awarded a gold medal for civic valor accompanied by the statement: "Sicilian businessman aware of the serious danger to which he was exposing himself, challenged the Mafia by publicly denouncing demands for extortion and by collaborating with the authorities in identifying the criminals. For this uncommon courage and for his constant dedication to opposing criminal blackmail he fell victim to an attack. A splendid example of moral integrity and of the highest civic virtues, driven to the extreme sacrifice."

14. It seems likely that Totò Riina thought Ignazio Salvo and Salvo Lima were both guilty of a terrible crime, that of having assured him the Maxi trial would come to nothing just as so many other legal actions in the past had come to nothing. He could expect to get a sentence in the first trial, but then over the course of the appeals process every accusation would drop away. But that's not the way it went.

On March 12, 1992, Lima got in his car to go to work. Traveling with him was the professor Alvredo Li Vecchi, with a colleague, Nando Liggio. Two men on a motorcycle shot at the car, breaking the windows, and aiming for only one target. Li Vecchi and Liggio were left unharmed as Salvo Lima got out of the car and desperately tried to flee on foot. He made it only a few feet before being hit.

Death came to Ignazio Salvo on September 17 of that same year.

15. Making his way toward the defendants' bench, Salvatore Riina suddenly turns and makes a gesture that is difficult to decipher, whether salute or warning. His arrest was one of the chapters of this story still difficult to understand, beginning with the discovery that the boss was hiding in a villa in Palermo, at Via Bernini, 52–54. On January 15, 1993, a special squad of the ROS (a special operational group), commanded by Sergio De Caprio, alias Captain Ultimo, intercepted Riina as he left home in a car. The delay between the time of his arrest and the search of the hideout became the source of great controversy since it was clear that members of the Cosa Nostra had profited from the delay to remove evidence and take away documents and other items sure to be of interest to the investigation. Captain De Caprio and his commander in the ROS, Mario Mori, were put under investigation and accused of aiding and abetting; they were acquitted in a judgment delivered in 2006 that was not appealed by the prosecutor's office.

10 The last godfathers

The RICO Act, John Gotti, and the Decline

His name was G. Robert Blakey, a lawyer and law professor at Notre Dame Law School, but he was still a student when he was drawn to the world of organized crime.

He was especially interested in the Apalachin meeting, when more than sixty mafiosi were stopped, about fifty managed to get away, and there was no chance to charge them with any crime.

During the sixties, with the supervision of Democratic senator John McClellan, Blakey drafted the RICO Act, a federal law enacted as part of the Organized Crime Control Act of 1970. RICO is an acronym for Racketeer Influenced and Corrupt Organization, a provision that made it possible to prosecute anyone who could be shown to belong to organized crime, introducing a criterion of objective responsibility.

It seems that the choice of "Rico" may reflect Blakey's passion for films, in particular for Edward G. Robinson in *Little Caesar*, where he plays a gangster named Rico. This is a notion Blakey has neither confirmed nor denied.

Like every new pronouncement, it took time for the RICO Act to be embraced by American prosecutors, resulting in a considerably long delay in its application. But once its potentials were understood, life for members of the American Mafia became truly difficult, so much so that John Gotti, who was arrested in 1990 and died in prison from throat cancer in 2002, can be said to have been the last true godfather in the history of the American Mafia.

At the dawn of the new millennium the Cosa Nostra families in the United States found themselves in great difficulty. Those in New York survived, but only with difficulty, as did those in Chicago and Miami, in some ways tied by common interests, but in the rest of the country the clans seemed to be on the point of dissolving and disappearing.

The reasons were many, beginning with the fact that many godfathers of the old generation were dead or had been arrested and given long prison sentences, and the new ranks still had not shown organizational skills even distantly comparable to those of their teachers. The same thing applied to the Mafia Commission, the organ of oversight and mediation founded by Lucky Luciano in 1931, today nearly dissolved and without leaders in circulation capable of refounding it.

The application of RICO, designed to permit the conviction of an individual solely on the basis of belonging to the Cosa Nostra, also convinced a good number of criminals to turn themselves into collaborators. Without a code of *omertà* comparable to that of their Sicilian cousins, and facing the prospect of never being able to get out of a federal prison, they preferred to deal with the FBI, helping to identify and dismantle illicit businesses, leading to the arrest of accomplices and companions, bartering their testimony for reduced sentences.

To this can be added the inevitable changes in society and its attitudes. The Cosa Nostra has always chosen its members from men of clear Italian descent, but city neighborhoods inhabited by only one ethnic group are no longer an aspect of urban reality. Recruitment is more difficult, the system of control of the lower-level soldiers is less effective, and the absolute veneration for bosses is nothing but a distant memory. Meanwhile Rudolph Giuliani, in his role as the zero-tolerance mayor of New York, passed administrative measures that prevented the Mafia from easy access to wholesale businesses or garbage disposal.

On the negative side, with the forces of the law ready for the final push, the Mafia found an unexpected ally in the tragedy of September 11. Resources that until then had been allocated for the struggle against organized crime were immediately withdrawn and redirected to deal with the far more urgent and threatening phenomenon of international terrorism.

Today the investigators and prosecutors involved in the battle against the Mafia number fewer than a quarter of those active before the attacks on the Twin Towers. And signs of danger were immediately noticed.

For example, between 2002 and 2005, members of the Bonanno family managed to organize illegal betting estimated at $360 million. Well aware that the thrill of betting money on winners and losers will never go out of style, the crime families not only continue to offer greater chances of winning (and without charging taxes on winnings), they also connect their illegal gambling operations to loansharking, another racket that does not go through crises. There is also the fact that the Colombo, Gambino, and Genovese families are again showing up at the worksites for large projects in New York, from the subway to the Museum of Modern Art to the new baseball stadium. Without the slightest embarrassment or shame, the underboss of the Lucchese family, Steven "Wonderboy" Crea, confessed to having extorted a bribe from the company hired to haul away debris from the Twin Towers, while representatives of the Bonanno family got busy in the collection of scrap metal from Ground Zero to resell on the black market.

The tangible risk the United State runs is exactly the same as that which Italy will face if the decision is made to let down the guard; silence from the Mafia should be interpreted as a strategy, not an absence.

While certain traditional ways of making money have waned, the Cosa Nostra has perfectly adapted to new situations, decidedly more modern and difficult to identify. Salvatore LoCascio of the Gambino family was accused of having pulled in more than $200 million in only five years by adding bogus charges to telephone bills.

Members of the Genovese family made more than $2.5 million a year duplicating compact discs on Long Island, while in Queens, with the complicity of clerks and shopkeepers, they have become involved in copying the credit cards of customers, once again setting up a multimillion-dollar business.

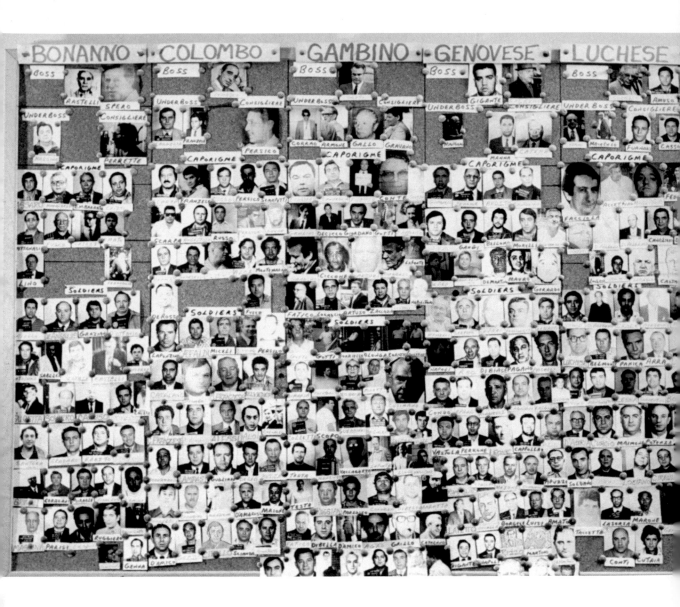

1. The photo above, taken during the eighties, shows a cork board with photos of all the mafiosi of the New York families, beginning with the bosses in the upper rows. The clans presented include, left to right, the Bonanno; the Colombo, with Carmine Persico at the top; the Gambino with John Gotti; the Genovese, directed by Vincent Gigante; and finally the Luchese (Lucchese), with their boss Anthony Carollo.

2. Paul Castellano, known as "Big Paulie," was born in Brooklyn on June 26, 1915, and served his first prison time at the age of nineteen. He joined the Mangano family and became a leader alongside Albert Anastasia. After Anastasia's murder the new boss, Carlo Gambino, wanted him beside him and named him his successor. However, know-ing Castellano's moderate tempera-ment, and for reasons of internal balance in the clan, Gambino made Big Paulie take Aniello "Neal" Dellacroce as his underboss. With-out renouncing violence entirely, Castellano was distinguished by his business skills, with a particular interest in the construction busi-ness and the property market.

3. In the eighties Castellano had to contend with the ambition of a young protégé of Aniello Dellacroce named John Gotti. In March of 1984 the threat came instead from the chief federal prosecutor of Manhattan Rudolph Giuliani, who indicted him using the RICO Act, the law expressly designed to strike at organized crime of the Mafia type. Arrested on charges of racketeering in 1985, Big Paulie was released on payment of $3 million bail, but there was word he had made a deal with the FBI.

On December 2, 1985, Dellacroce died of lung cancer, and on the sixteenth John Gotti ordered the elimination of Castellano. That same day, in front of the Sparks Steak House in Manhattan, the boss of the Gambino family and his faithful new underboss, Thomas "Tommy" Bilotti, fell under the bullets of Gotti's hit men.

4. Vincent Gigante (1928–2005) was known as the "Chin" because of a particularly pronounced physical feature. He also had a flattened nose, but that was the result of his early career as a professional fighter, which he performed with moderate success from 1944 to 1947.

Salvatore and Yolanda Gigante had five sons, and aside from the one who became a priest all the others ended up as mafiosi in the Genovese family. Vince, however, had something more, for which reason, in 1957, he was involved in the failed assassination of Frank Costello.

His ascent in the family was unstoppable, and when John Gotti and other leaders of the Gambino family were arrested in 1992 he became the most powerful boss in New York.

Fearing incrimination and prosecution, Gigante as early as 1969 adopted the curious strategy of pretending to be crazy: he wandered through the streets of Greenwich Village dressed in slippers and a robe mumbling to himself. Despite his dedication to this performance, in the end the Chin was convicted in 1997 of racketeering and sentenced to twelve years in prison. He died behind bars on December 19, 2005.

5. He could be taken for a modern version of Al Capone. There is the same arrogance, the same icy ferocity, but most of all the narcissism, which led him to scan the newspapers every day to see how many times his name appeared. Nicodemo Domenico Scarfo, "Little Nicky" to his friends, was born in Brooklyn in 1929 and soon became part of the Philadelphia family, directed first by Joseph Ida and then by Angelo Bruno. It was Bruno who sent Scarfo to Atlantic City, where Nicky revealed his undoubted talents as a gangster; when Bruno was killed, Scarfo took over the family. The problems with the law that closed his criminal career arose at the end of the eighties. Scarfo today is in the U.S. penitentiary in Atlanta serving a sentence that runs to 2033, by which time Little Nicky will have reached his 104th birthday.

6. Rudolph Giuliani has Italian roots, with grandparents from Montecatini Terme in Tuscany. He was born in Brooklyn in May 1944 and became famous as the zero-tolerance mayor of New York City. In 1983 Giuliani was appointed U.S. attorney for the Southern District of New York. He thus found himself investigating enterprises and activities clearly related to the Gambino family. In fighting organized crime, and later as mayor of New York, his model was Fiorello La Guardia. He met Giovanni Falcone and Paolo Borsellino, with whom he collaborated on the investigations of the Cosa Nostra's international trafficking.

7. His image seemed to be that of a classic mafioso: always wearing a fedora, cigar clenched between his teeth, a body that merited the nickname "Fat Tony." But Anthony Salerno (1911–1992), shown opposite in an image from 1985, was not merely a caricature. Born and raised in Harlem, he spent his entire career in the Genovese family, becoming its boss in 1981. In reality, Salerno was the "front boss," with the more energetic Vincent Gigante always behind him. Fat Tony managed to keep himself out of prison for a long time, but in 1985 he was caught and the next year he was convicted. The sentence was hard, almost a century of imprisonment, but he served only six years. Suffering from diabetes, with suspected prostate cancer, he died of a stroke at the Medical Center for Federal Prisoners in Springfield, Missouri, on July 27, 1992.

8. His name was Carmine Galante. The photo shows him on the ground, having fallen off the chair, his body crumpled, the cigar still in his mouth, his blood on the pavement. He had just finished eating at Joe and Mary's, a restaurant in Brooklyn, when they shot him in the face and chest.

The sixty-nine-year-old boss was killed on July 12, 1979, by a group of killers hired by Alphonse "Sonny Red" Indelicato, a man of honor in the Bonanno family. Richard Kuklinski, perhaps the most famous of the Mafia's contract killers (in the photo opposite), also claimed to have taken part in the hit. But the autopsy report on Galante's body seems to contradict his claim, showing that Galante was killed with a shotgun, not the handgun Kuklinksi said he'd used.

9. Richard Kuklinski was born in Jersey City, New Jersey, on April 11, 1935. A psychopath, he was a murderer who enjoyed torturing and killing. In a television interview he himself told of at least a hundred murders he'd committed before the Mafia discovered his "talent," hiring him for its dirtiest work. He was known as the "Iceman," not so much for his coldness as for his habit of freezing the bodies of his victims to prevent law enforcement doctors from calculating the time of death. By the time he was captured, thanks to an informer, he had committed more than two hundred murders. In 1988 he was found guilty of five murders; it was impossible to find witnesses to any other crimes. On March 5, 2006, Kuklinksi died of natural causes in the Trenton prison at age seventy-one.

10–11. He was called the "Dapper Don," although some suggest the correct nickname for John Joseph Gotti Jr. (on the right below) was the "Teflon Don," since accusations never seemed to stick to the leader of the Gambino family. But Gotti went too far, felt invincible, a little like Capone, like Luciano, and the FBI took advantage, planting bugs in his rooms and in the telephones he used.

Born in 1940 in New York City, he took leadership of the family after eliminating its boss, Paul Castellano, in December 1985. He trusted his own intuition, the ability to intimidate or fascinate anyone near him, first among them his underboss Salvatore "Sammy the Bull" Gravano (opposite).

When Gotti was arrested on December 11, 1990, together with Gravano, he wasn't overly concerned, but he had failed to take into account the Bull, to whom the FBI made a winning offer: freedom and entrance in the Witness Protection Program in return for treason. The sentence put the Dapper Don behind bars forever, with no possibility of parole.

On June 10, 2002, John Gotti died from throat cancer in the same medical center in Springfield, Missouri, where Tony Salerno had died ten years earlier.

12. This photograph, taken in a New York City restaurant in November 2003, shows Frank Calì to the left, Nicola Mandalà of the Villabate family in the center, with the young Gianni Nicchi, of the Pagliarelli clan, to the right.

Francesco Paolo Augusto Calì, known as "Franky Boy," was born in New York in 1965 and soon married a girl from the Inzerillo family, with whom he had two children. In the nineties he was taken into the Gambino family, becoming to all effects a man of honor and later assuming an operative role. His cover for being in New York was his involvement in the Circuit Fruits supermarket chain. His contacts with the Sicilian Mafia, as well as with the 'Ndrangheta of Siderno, were interrupted when he was arrested in February 2008 within the sphere of Operation Old Bridge.

13. Pietro Inzerillo, known as "Tall Pete," is a member of the Gambino family implicated in the Old Bridge operation. Age forty-three, in June 2010, he was taken with a new arrest warrant issued by the district attorney of New York. Together with several accomplices he was accused of having taken illegal sports bets and having been involved in criminal usury and extortion, for an annual volume of business amounting to $20 million.

14. Giovanni (left) is the son of Salvatore Inzerillo, killed in May 1981 by hit men sent by Riina during the Second Mafia War, and that was not the only drama of his life. Although only fourteen, his brother, Giuseppe, swore he would exact revenge for their father's murder but was kidnapped and tortured by Pino Greco, who hacked off his right arm—which he had sworn he would use to kill Riina—before shooting him.

Born in Brooklyn on April 30, 1972, and officially a construction entrepreneur, Giovanni went to Italy in 2000. He lives in the house at 346 Via Castellana in the Passo di Rigano quarter of Palermo where his father lived before being killed. He too was arrested on February 7, 2008, during Operation Old Bridge.

15–16. Roberto Settineri was the link joining the Corso family of Palermo to the Gambino and Colombo clans in New York. He lived in the United States until 1998, making a home in Miami. Officially, he worked as an importer and distributor of Italian wines, but in reality he was involved in a far more lucrative relationship with Gaetano and Thomas Napoli and with Frankie Di Stefano, a man of honor near the leader of the Gambinos, Joseph Corozzo. He loved to act like a boss, with a cigar always clamped between his lips, and in honor of one of the world's most poplar television series about the Mafia he decided to open a bar and call it the Soprano Café. But Settineri was also a man attentive to progress, so much so that he used Skype in his communications with his business associates, a tool that made wiretapping difficult. Despite his passion for technology, a banal telephone call to Gioacchino Corso, recorded in 2005, opened the way for the investigation that ended in Operation Paesan Blues, on March 10, 2010, an operation that included his arrest.

17. Peter Gotti, known as "One-Eyed Pete" because glaucoma left him with only one seeing eye, is the older brother of the defunct John. Born in New York City in 1939, Peter Gotti joined the Gambino family in the sixties, but only in 1988 was he taken in as a full-fledged member of the clan. In reality, his brother John never believed he had the ability to grow inside the Cosa Nostra and relegated him to completely marginal positions. But when John and his lieutenants ended up in prison, Peter proved himself to be a useful figure and, along with Nicholas Corozzo and John D'Amico, took care of the Gambino family affairs.

In June 2002, a few days before John's death, Peter Gotti was indicted on racketeering charges and extortion (his victims included the actor Steven Seagal); then, in 2004, he was charged with plotting to eliminate several police informants, among them Salvatore "Sammy the Bull" Gravano. Despite imprisonment, it seems that Peter Gotti still maintains his position of boss in the Gambino family, albeit without exercising any operational role.

18. On the left is Joe DeCicco, on the right John "Jackie the Nose" D'Amico, in the middle is John Gotti's son, John Angelo Gotti III, best known as "Junior" Gotti. Jackie is today the number two in the Gambino clan, but the youngest of the Gotti family, born in 1964, has never been fully appreciated.

An event that occurred in 1997 may explain this. Looking through one of Junior's properties the FBI discovered $350,000 in cash, a list of the guests to his wedding accompanied by the dollar value of their gifts, two guns, and, best of all, a list of the members of the family. From then on, the local media called him *dumbfella*, or worse, claiming the young man didn't merit the name *goodfella*.

After a series of run-ins with the law, on the threshold of age fifty, Junior declared he'd quit the Mafia and wanted to dedicate himself to writing children's books.

19. Nicholas Corozzo's parents came from a town near Cuneo, but "Little Nick," as he was called, was born in Brooklyn in 1940. Loyal to his boss John Gotti, even though he did not promote him within the family, Corozzo created an illegal betting operation in the nineties using various websites in the United States and Costa Rica. After the arrest of John D'Amico as part of Operation Old Bridge, Corozzo assumed command of the family for a few months. Included on the list of the ten most wanted criminals in America, Little Nick turned himself in on May 29, 2008. Sentenced for enterprise corruption and sports betting, he will finish serving his time in March 2020.

21. Dominick Cirillo, called the "Quiet Dom," was born in East Harlem in July 1929. His father, Alphonse, served as a man of honor to the then boss of the Profaci family, Joseph Magliocco.

Aside from his criminal activities, one of the factors that most affects his life is his passion for boxing, which led him to meet both Thomas Eboli and Vincent "the Chin" Gigante. Cirillo owes his role in the Genoese clan primarily to Gigante, and when the Chin was arrested in 1997 the command passed to a committee called the Administration, coordinated by Cirillo. Having served most of a four-year sentence for racketeering, he was released in August 2008 at the age of seventy-nine and today occupies the position of consigliere.

20. Salvatore Montagna, known as "Sal the Iron Worker," is an anomalous figure in the Cosa Nostra world. Still comparatively young, he was born in Montreal in 1971, grew up at Castellammare del Golfo, and arrived with his family in the Bronx when already a boy. Little is known of how he joined the Mafia, but around the end of the nineties he became part of the Bonanno family under the guidance of Joe Massino. Since 2008 the FBI has believed Montagna to be the acting boss of the Bonanno clan.

In 2009, after the U.S. immigration services discovered he did not possess American citizenship, the Iron Worker was deported to Canada, his country of origin.

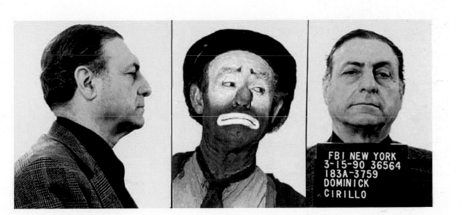

22. Venero Mangano, known as "Benny Eggs" because his mother ran an egg farm, is one of the oldest bosses in circulation. Born in 1921, related to the ex-leader of the Gambino family, Vincent Mangano, he served with honor during the Second World War, earning a Distinguished Flying Cross. Released in 2006 after serving a sentence of fifteen years for murder, Mangano was thought to be the underboss of the Genovese family.

23. It can be said that Carmine Persico Jr. was born to his profession: his father was a man of honor tied to Lucky Luciano.

Carmine the "Snake," or the "Immortal," was born in Brooklyn on August 8, 1937, and entered the Colombo family when only twenty, wanted by the boss of the time, Joe Profaci. At the beginning of the seventies, with the death of Joseph Colombo, Persico became the boss of the Colombo family, a position he still occupies. Today, he is currently serving a life sentence for murder and racketeering.

24–25. Vittorio "Little Vic" Amuso (right) was born in Queens in 1934 in an area under control of the Lucchese family, which he joined at the end of the forties. Bodyguard of Carmine Tramunti, he was taken into the family at the end of the fifties, supported by Joseph "Crazy Joe" Gallo. Since 2009 he has been considered the boss of the Lucchese family and is currently in prison with a life sentence for murder and racketeering charges.

Matthew "Matt" Madonna (at left in the photo to the left), a year younger, is one of the men nearest Amuso, who wanted him to be acting boss together with Aniello "Neil" Migliore and Joseph "Joey Dee" DiNapoli. In October 2009 Madonna, along with Joseph DiNapoli and twenty-seven others, was indicted for being the central element in a vast network of extortion, loansharking, and arms traffic, with an income of more than $400 million annually.

26. At age fifty-two Carmen DiNunzio didn't look much like a dangerous man; even his nickname got more grins than shivers—"Big Cheese"—with the tabloids even more caustic, calling him "the god-father of Gorgonzola." Despite his size, since 2005 DiNunzio has been the underboss of the New England Mafia family, one of the most active in the United States; recently his name has been associated with Mafia infiltrations in the Big Dig, the colossal plan that called for construction of an underground tunnel through the city of Boston.

27–28. Joseph Anthony Ligambi (left), called "Uncle Joe," was born in Philadelphia in August 1939 and is today the boss of the Philadelphia family, which he joined in 1986.

At the time the family was controlled by Nicodemo Scarfo, who took control after the murder of Angelo Bruno. Both Scarfo and Ligambi received prison sentences for the murder of the gambler Frank D'Alfonso, and leadership of the family was assumed by Joseph Merlino.

Ligambi's conviction was overturned, Merlino was arrested, and in 2001 Ligambi became the boss of the family. His leadership has been calm and subdued, turning away from flamboyance and violence and managing to revive the clan, which had reached the threshold of extinction. Marty Angelina (photo at far left) is the effective underboss, and unlike his boss he is often in the limelight because of the distracting if futile excesses of his behavior.

11 From Massacres to Crisis

The Attack on the State and the Response from Institutions

From the time of the First Mafia War, the winning faction of the Cosa Nostra has been the one that holds superior firepower, able to field the most vicious hit men, the most efficient death squads. The price was paid by the Bontate and Inzerillo families, by the families of Buscetta and Marino Mannoia, but the dead also included loyal civil servants along with those citizens who were simply unwilling to accept the wall of *omertà* and who publicly reported the crimes of the Cosa Nostra.

During the eighties the Anti-Mafia Pool of Palermo judges and the Maxi trial marked the turning point in the struggle against the Mafia, and the Corleonesi, commanded by Totò Riina, responded with an unprecedented counterattack. They unleashed a season of slaughters.

In 1992 Giovanni Falcone, his wife, and his three bodyguards were murdered at Capaci; Paolo Borsellino and the five agents who accompanied him everywhere died on Palermo's Via D'Amelio. In 1993 the violence knew no bounds, with attacks in Rome and carnage in Florence and Milan. Terrible episodes, these were political Mafia crimes of which we know the perpetrators but not who sent them.

If Riina's aim was to get some sort of deal from the institutions, to force them by means of intimidation to revise laws and processes, the result he obtained seems to have been the exact opposite: thousands of citizens took to the streets in protest, and the state unleashed the operation code-named Sicilian Vespers, sending twenty thousand soldiers to Sicily to take charge of sensitive targets, thus freeing the *carabineri* and police from that role and allowing them to return to their investigative functions.

In January 1993 Totò Riina was arrested; in 1995 it was Leoluca Bagarella, and the next year Giovanni Brusca. At that point, direction of the Corleonesi passed into the hands of the fugitive Bernardo Provenzano, who made a sharp change in direction, attempting a low profile and silence and no more "excellent cadavers," as well as a ban on excessive violence, including the violence inside the criminal organization itself. Under Provenzano's direction, the Mafia returned to what it was during the sixties, so invisible it gave the impression of having disappeared.

This was obviously nothing more than a tactical move, for if it is true that the Sicilian Mafia is not as powerful as it was in the past, if it can no longer count on the incredible earnings of the nineties guaranteed by the international traffic in drugs, it still has not lost control of its territory.

On April 11, 2006, after forty-three years as a fugitive, Provenzano was captured in a farmhouse near Corleone. In the same place the investigators found other precious materials, above all the famous *pizzini*, small scraps of paper with the encrypted messages the boss had used for years to communicate with his inner circle.

On June 20, 2006, Operation Gotha was unleashed, with fifty-two arrest warrants and five hundred policemen involved, and the three men who had directed the Mafia following the arrest of Provenzano ended up in handcuffs. The three were Nino Rotolo, boss of the Pagliarelli area of Palermo; Antonino Cinà, formerly personal physician to both Riina and Provenzano; and the builder Franco Bonura, tied to the Uditore family.

On November 5, 2007, after twenty-five years of being a fugitive, the boss Salvatore Lo Piccolo, the presumed successor to Provenzano, was arrested.

With Riina, Bagarella, and Provenzano in prison, and the leaders of the Corleonsi decapitated, the survivors of the Inzerillo family found themselves faced with the opportunity to return to Italy. At the time of the *mattanza*, with Salvatore Inzerillo and many other members of the family killed, the remaining survivors took flight to the United States, thanks in part to relatives among the Gambino family.

Riina had agreed to give up on tracking them down and killing them provided they agreed that neither they nor their offspring would ever return to Sicily. Since then the *scappati* ("escapees"), as they were called, had limited their business to the new world.

Operation Old Bridge began on February 7, 2008, a joint action of the FBI and the Direzione Anti-Mafia; between New York and Sicily ninety people were arrested, among them Giovanni Inzerillo, Frank Calì, officially a businessman for Italian Food Distribution, and Filippo Casamento. Nicholas Corozzo, head of the Gambino family, managed to escape the roundup but turned himself in on May 29; another who got away, Gianni Nicchi, was captured in Palermo in December of 2009. Operation Old Bridge ended the nascent plan of the Inzerillo clan to regain its former power at the heights of the Cosa Nostra.

Investigative successes followed one another at a rate never before recorded, and on December 16, 2008, came Operation Perseo, in the course of which *carabinieri* arrested roughly a hundred Palermo mafiosi, thwarting the plan, supported by the fugitive Matteo Messina Denaro, to reconstruct Palermo's provincial Commission. Operation Paesan Blues, which began on March 10, 2010, ended in July with arrest warrants for Giocchino and Gianpaolo Corso, along with other members of the Santa Maria di Gesù and Porta Nuova Mafia families. Paesan Blues demonstrated once again the business ties between the Sicilian Cosa Nostra and the American Mafia. A figure of central importance to the relationship was Roberto Settineri, a Palermitan who went to Miami to direct an import-export wine business but was in reality the Sicilian mediator of the Gambino and Colombo families.

The pressure being applied by police officers and anti-Mafia prosecutors seems strong, but experience teaches that the Mafia knows how to avoid or survive frontal assaults and does not stop weaving its web, much like a spider whose web is destroyed.

The next moves are difficult to predict. Cosa Nostra might move on to the successors of Riina and Provenzano, entrusting the command to the fugitive from Trapani Matteo Messina Denaro. Or it might make a sharp change in direction, dropping its hierarchal structure in favor of something less rigid, on the model of the Calabrian 'Ndrangheta, today the most powerful criminal organization in Italy and one of the strongest in the world.

1–2. These two photographs go far beyond simple documentation because of their symbolic value and their emotional charge. Opposite is Totò Riina after his arrest in 1993, sitting alone with his thoughts, perhaps trying to think up ways to limit the damage, maintain control, or even get revenge on those who did not live up to his expectations.

Hanging on the wall above him is a portrait of General Dalla Chiesa, a man who gave his life in the battle against Riina and the criminals like him, a hero let down by the state he served, which failed to provide him with the solid support he needed precisely at the moment in which it was most important for such institutions to demonstrate solid unity.

The same destiny awaited two friends, two great men the public's imagination has molded into a single being: the judges Giovanni Falcone (left) and Paolo Borsellino, shown together below.

3–4. Francesca Morvillo and Giovanni Falcone got married in May of 1986. They met during the season of poisons, a bitter moment in Falcone's career, and some of his colleagues were quick to point out to him that his relationship with Francesca, who was also a magistrate in Palermo, was not necessarily a good idea. But he and Francesca had nothing to hide, only a beautiful story of the love of life. That life had to be lived in the constant company of bodyguards, the only exception being when they were on a boat, spent with constant work that seemed more like a mission than work, without even the idea of children since the danger was just too great to even think about.

Francesca Laura Morvillo outlived her husband by only five hours, following the Mafia attack known as the Capaci massacre on May 23, 1992, when Giovanni Brusca pressed the remote-control detonator that set off the bomb as the cars of the judges and their escort drove over it. Three members of the escort died with Falcone and his wife. Their names were Vito Schifani, Rocco Dicillo, and Antonio Montinaro.

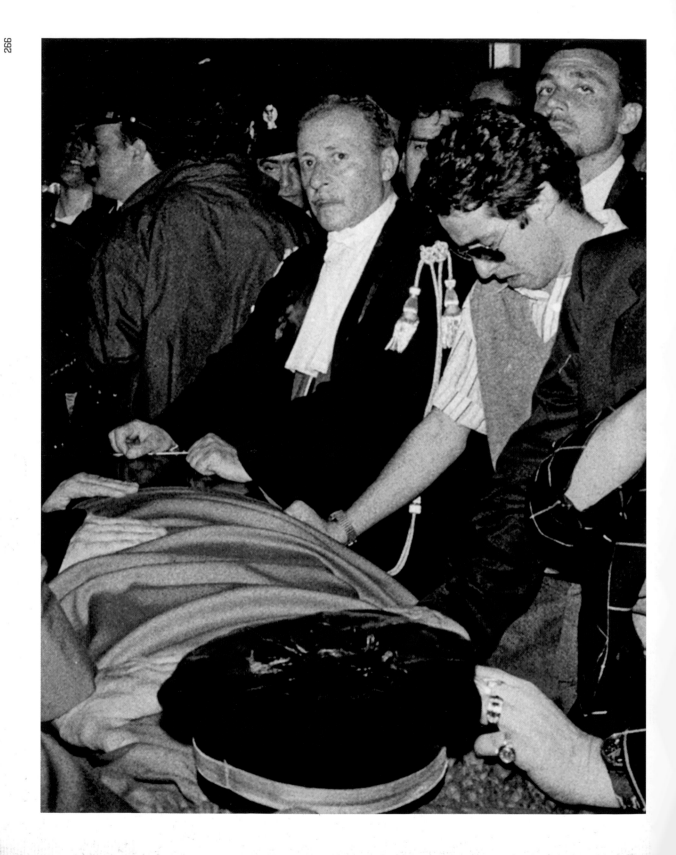

5–6. There is desperation in the face of Paolo Borsellino (center), his hands resting on the coffin of his friend Giovanni. There is the awareness of being himself a target, such that he had been telling his friends and colleagues that he could not stop, he had to dedicate all his energy to investigations and files because there was no more time.

Born in Palermo on January 19, 1940, he grew up in the La Kalsa quarter, the same as Giovanni Falcone and also Tommaso Buscetta. After getting his law degree he passed the judiciary examination in 1963. In 1980 Rocco Chinnici had the idea of creating the Anti-Mafia Pool, which put together judges like Falcone, Borsellino, Giuseppe Di Lello, Leonardo Guarnotta, and Giovanni Barrile and enabled them to work together with police officials such as Ninni Cassarà and Beppe Montana.

Fifty-seven days after the Capaci massacre, while paying a visit to his elderly mother in Palermo's Via D'Amelio, a car bomb killed Borsellino and five members of his escort: Agostino Catalano, Emanuela Loi, Vincenzo Li Muli, Walter Cosina, and Claudio Traina. In a television interview given twenty days before his death Borsellino had said, "I know that all of us have the moral duty to continue our work and to do so without being influenced by the sensation—or, I would say, by the certainty—that all of this may cost us dearly."

7. The results of the Maxi trial, with the later confirmation of sentences at various levels of appeal, plus the application of Article 41-bis prison regime, which limited a mafioso's ability to run operations from behind bars, drove the Corleonesi to a ferocious response. The night between 26 and 27 May, 1993, a car laden with explosives blew up in Via dei Georgofili in Florence (photo below). Five people died, among them a nine-year-old girl and a newborn girl only fifty days old. Two months later Mafia-style attacks took place in Rome and most of all in Milan, where on July 27, on Via Palestro in the heart of the city, a car bomb killed another five people, including three firemen and a policeman.

8. Giuseppe "Pino" Puglisi (1937–1993) knew the meaning of poverty and how easy it was to slide into crime. He knew because he was born in the Brancaccio quarter of Palermo, because his father was a shoemaker, his mother a dressmaker, and because he chose to become a priest on the street, living directly among the people. He never quit preaching against crime and criminals, and in 1990 he was made the parish priest of his birthplace, the Brancaccio quarter, the territory ruled by the Graviano brothers, who were faithful not to the teachings of the church but only to Leoluca Bagarella.

They shot him to death on the street on September 15, 1993. When the killers pointed their pistols at him he smiled and spoke his last words, "I've been expecting you." The shooter was Salvatore Grigoli, and with him was Gaspare Spatuzza; they'd been sent by Filippo and Giuseppe Graviano. Six years after his death, the process to beatify Puglisi began, while his favorite question had become graffiti on Palermo's walls: "And what if somebody did something?"

9–10. Michele Graviano was killed in 1982 in a feud between rival gangs. The family tradition was carried on by his four sons, most of all Filippo and Giuseppe, the bosses of Brancaccio, shown here after their arrest on January 27, 1994 (Giuseppe is on the right).

Involved in the deaths of Falcone and Borsellino, then in the attacks in Florence and Milan, as well as being behind the murder of the priest Puglisi, the Gravianos profited from their time behind bars to earn degrees, one in economics and one in mathematics, a sign that ignorance and cruelty do not always go hand in hand. More recently a sensation was caused by the declarations of a *pentito*, Antonino Giuffrè, supported by another collaborator, Gaspare Spatuzza, who claimed the Gravianos had acted as intermediaries between the Mafia and the highest members of Forza Italia, Silvio Berlusconi's party. On December 11, 2009, Filippo Graviano denied Spatuzza's statements.

The controversy unleashed by this is far from over while everyone waits to see if the judges find or fail to find sure confirmation of the revelations of the two collaborators.

11. The number of victims of the Mafia is frightening. It includes those killed because they were trying to put mafiosi behind the bars of a prison, those who refused to give in to Mafia blackmail, those who lost their lives in clashes between rival gangs, in the struggle among criminals, where what counts is being the strongest or the quickest. Along with spectacular executions and the murders that are committed in public to send a message while eliminating an enemy, there is a more subtle way of striking, the so-called *lupara bianca* ("white shotgun" because there is no blood), in which the victim is killed and made to disappear forever, leaving no body. Every so often a Mafia cemetery is discovered, such as in the case shown above. Visible in this photograph, which dates to 1994, are human remains found in a cave near Rocca Busambra, the highest peak of the Monti Sicani, between Palermo and Agrigento.

12. Giuseppe Di Matteo was thirteen and had a passion for horses. He also had a problem called Santino, his father. In 1993 Santino became an informant and gave information about the bomb that killed Falcone and the others at Capaci, although he did not take part in the attack. He later decided to break with the Corleonesi clan and collaborate with the law. So the Corleonesi kidnapped Giuseppe, who became the small victim of indirect revenge. Santino thought it over. He didn't want harm to come to his son, but at the same time he didn't want to stop talking to the judges. On January 11, 1996, after 779 days as a prisoner, Giuseppe was strangled to death and his body dissolved in a barrel of acid.

13. "I killed Giovanni Falcone. But it wasn't the first time: I had already used car bombs to kill Judge Rocco Chinnici and the men of his escort. I'm responsible for the kidnapping and death of little Giuseppe Di Matteo, who was thirteen when he was taken and fifteen when he was killed. I committed and ordered personally more than one hundred fifty crimes. Even today I can't remember all the names of those I killed. Many more than a hundred, definitely less than two hundred."

Such was the declaration of Giovanni Brusca, known as the *Scannacristiani*, son of the boss Bernardo Brusca, whom he succeeded in 1989 as capo-mandamento of the San Giuseppe Jato clan. He was arrested in Agrigento on May 20, 1996. Since 2000 he has been collaborating with the law.

14. He was called 'u Signurinu (the "Little Gentleman") because of his habits and style, but there was nothing of the dandy about Pietro Aglieri, over the years becoming one of the most merciless men in the Cosa Nostra, the capo-mandamento of Santa Maria del Gesù, made powerful through an alliance with the Corleonesi during the Second Mafia War. He was arrested on June 6, 1997. Aglieri was one of those criminals for whom devotion to the church and its precepts did not constitute an insurmountable block to slaughters and murders. In the hideout where he had hidden for years investigators found space set aside for a small votive shrine.

He was condemned to life in prison for the murder of Judge Antonio Scopelliti (1935–1991) as well as for the Capaci massacre.

15–16–17. Bernardo Provenzano led the Corleonesi after the arrest of Riina, in 1993, and he became the principal reference after Bagarella and Brusca were captured, respectively in 1995 and 1996. Provenzano preferred a strategy different from that of Riina: no more frontal clashes; he wanted to lower the volume, slow the rhythm, pretend to be dead or at least gravely wounded. He was difficult to track down, so much so that he holds the record among mafiosi for the length of time he was a fugitive—more than forty years. Complicated investigative work led to the discovery that in 2002 he had undergone a surgical operation in Marseille, and this made it possible to extract samples of his DNA that would have proven useful had he undergone plastic surgery to change his appearance. The interception of the *pizzini* (such as the example at lower right), and then identification of the food and laundry services that made deliveries to him, enabled the men of Palermo's flying squad and the Servizio Centrale Operative to identify the farmhouse near Corleone (above right) where the boss was hiding. On April 11, 2006, following ten days spent monitoring the situation, the blitz was unleashed. Provenzano did not make any reaction and confirmed his identity.

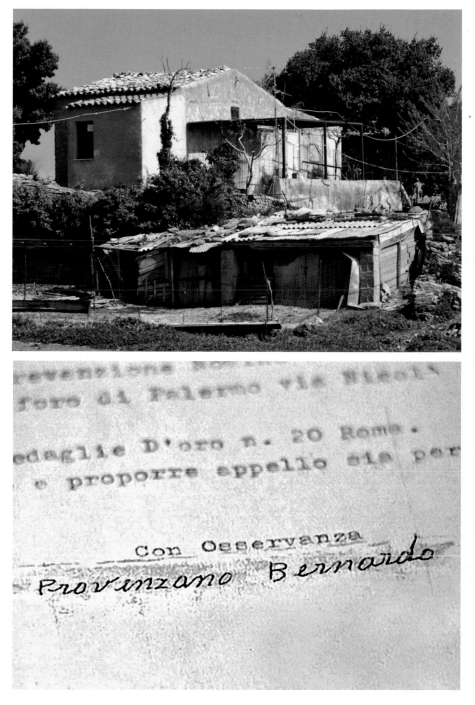

18–19. On June 20, 2006, as part of Operation Gotha, the prosecutor's office of Palermo issued fifty-two arrest warrants for mafiosi. Those arrested included Rosario (above) and Tommaso Inzerillo (below). The Inzerillo family's story is dramatic since they were forced to flee to the United States after the murder of Totuccio and the Second Mafia War. Even though they were winning, the Corleonesi did not let up, and to avoid being killed Tommaso chose to betray, eliminating two members of his own family who had fled to America. His cousin Antonio disappeared into nothingness, victim of a *lupara bianca*, in October 1981. The body of his uncle Pietro Inzerillo was found on January 15, 1982, in the trunk of a sports car parked in front of the Hilton Mount Laurel hotel in New Jersey. There was a $5 bill stuck in the dead man's mouth and two singles over his genitals, emblematic of his scarce value as a man. The car was registered to Joe's Pizza of Philadelphia.

20–21. Salvatore Lo Piccolo (above) was called the "Baron"; a fugitive since 1983, he was a thorn in the side of the special section of Palermo's flying squad called Catturandi (from the word for "capture"). He was seen as a man of great power, capable of forming strategic alliances with Bernardo Provenzano, Matteo Messina Denaro, and the bosses of the Cosa Nostra in the United States. He was finally taken on November 5, 2007, together with his son Sandro (left), Andrea Adamo, and Gaspare Pulizzi.

When the agents looked through the seized documents they found a kind of guide to being a member of the Mafia with a list of ten commandments.

1. No one can present himself directly to another of our friends. There must be a third person to do it.

2. Never look at the wives of friends.

3. Never be seen with cops.

4. Don't go to bars and clubs.

5. It is a duty to always be available for Cosa Nostra. Even if your wife is about to give birth.

6. Appointments must always be respected.

7. Wives must be treated with respect.

8. When asked for any information, the answer must always be the truth.

9. Money cannot be appropriated if it belongs to other Mafia members or families.

10. People who cannot be part of Cosa Nostra: anyone who has a close relative in the police; anyone with a two-timing relative in the family; anyone who behaves badly and doesn't hold to moral values.

22. Domenico Raccuglia, known as Mimmo, was born October 27, 1964, at Altofonte, of which he became boss, as well as capo-mandamento of San Giuseppe Jato and Partinico. After the arrest of Provenzano and Lo Piccolo, Mimmo saw himself as the new leader of the Sicilian Cosa Nostra. There were others, however, who didn't think he was old enough or had enough charisma to take over. In any case, his dream of glory didn't last long because the police arrested him on November 15, 2008, in Calatafimi, in the province of Trapani. He found himself facing three life sentences: first for a series of crimes committed in the nineties, second for the murder of Girolamo La Barbera, and third for the death of the young Giuseppe Di Matteo.

23. Giovanni Nicchi, known as Gianni, was called 'u Picciuittedu (the "Little Boy") because he was not yet thirty years old. However, following the arrests of Provenzano and then of Antonio Rotolo, Nicchi's godfather and mentor, Nicchi proved old enough to become the *reggente* ("regent") of the Pagliarelli man-damento. He was on the list used by Operation Gotha, sought for extortion and association with the Mafia, but he managed to escape arrest. He stayed at large until December 5, 2008, when the police struck a hard blow at the new Mafia, capturing him in an apartment house in Via Juvarra, Palermo, and at the same time, in Milan, capturing Gaetano Fidanzati, the seventy-five-year-old boss of the Acquasanta family and one of the most |important criminals in the international drug ring.

The Mafia Is Not Defeated

Conclusion by Pietro Grasso, Italy's National Anti-Mafia Prosecutor

Matteo Messina Denaro is forty-eight years old and the rules of the Mafia are written in his DNA, for he's the son of Don Ciccio, capo-mandamento of Castelvetrano. Denaro (photo opposite) is sought for criminal association, murder, and massacre. Called 'u Siccu (the "Skinny One"), or more recently, in the pizzini exchanged with Bernardo Provenzano, "Alessio," he is the most famous fugitive in Italy and beyond, for which reason he merits a place in Forbes's list of the World's 10 Most Wanted Fugitives. But the Mafia is not limited to Matteo Messina Denaro.

It would be a serious error to reduce it to one man or even to a few. And although the police, in collaboration with the justice system, have delivered powerful blows to the organization, it would be equally dangerous to believe that the Mafia is on the ropes, that it has been defeated.

The Mafia is there even if it doesn't shoot, even if it doesn't blow up cars packed with TNT, even if it doesn't strike in broad daylight, killing people like Dalla Chiesa, Falcone, or Borsellino. Those who believe otherwise are ingenuous or, what is certainly far worse, have some interest in inducing others to believe it.

Today's Mafia has embraced an old Sicilian proverb, "Calati iuncu ca passa la china," literally, "Bend over, reed, and let the flood waters pass," meaning wait and put up with it so you won't be broken and, when better times come, you'll be able to straighten up again.

As happened after the First Mafia War, after the Ciaculli massacre, and before the rise of the Corleonesi, the Mafia is seeking to make itself invisible. But it is still highly active and dangerous while it seeks to relaunch its role both in the economic sector and in those political and institutional. For the Mafia, this is not a time to seek open confrontations; it is instead a time to control violence, putting mediation in the foreground, reestablishing relationships with politicians, with the economy, with institutions.

The strategy of invisibility can, however, present another advantage, from the point of view of an unexpressed but intuitable exchange: the renouncing of aggression, the ensurance of a sort of peaceful coexistence with those who hold power; the decrease in problems of public order and security make it easier, almost automatic, to satisfy the aspirations of the mafiosi on various themes, such as the bringing about of a system of guarantees that will inevitably ensure them of a hefty dose of impunity.

Throughout all of its history the Mafia has never wed a political party, seeking instead to weave relationships with whomever, at the historical moment, happens to be leading the nation. And this applies to the modern trend for bipolar systems and alternation.

The Mafia has no ideologies if not that of feeding itself and its power to the detriment of any other structure or institution it can parasitize.

What counts is that no democratic change can ever be made in Italy while the Mafia and those with political power vie for the consensus of the people through a subtle game of intimidation, blackmail, patronage, and interests that are often convergent. There can be no progress while relationships exist among mafiosi, politicians, and businessmen with the goal of appropriating public funds and using them to take part in lucrative schemes.

The Mafia fears one thing, as much as and sometimes more than repression: attacks on the terrain of communication and social action, for hostility and ill repute prevent mafiosi from acquiring the consensus that is indispensable for them to act within civil society.

Therefore it is not enough to oppose the Mafia with police actions. Italians must talk about democracy and then bring it into being, in both the south and the rest of the country. "Democracy" must not remain an empty concept, a hope, but must be instead a solid base of active participation, with the involvement of citizens but also of all those who represent them in parties, in politics, in institutions, in unions, in movements, in trade associations.

The anti-Mafia of repressions must move alongside the anti-Mafia of healthy politics and finances, of efficiency in public administration, of well-functioning schools. Only in that way can a government, a state, merit the faith of its citizens and not reduce the struggle against the Mafia to a war of the good against the bad. Because the struggle against the Mafia means the struggle for the conquest of freedom, of democracy, of greater social justice.

The magistrates and the forces of order do not spare themselves, have never spared themselves, and proof of this are the dozens of dead who have paid for their dedication. It is up to all institutions and to civil society to make a leap forward in quality, to move from emotion to planning.

The culture of participation is the exact opposite of the culture of delegating, and the processes of liberation cannot be achieved by delegating but through involvement every day, on both a personal level and the group level. The culture of legality goes beyond the simple observance of laws and rules and is based on principles, ideas, behaviors directed at the creation of the rights and values of the person, of the dignity of each human, of the ideal of freedom, equality, democracy, truth, and justice.

Legality is the strength of the weak, the strength of the victims of abuses and violence, of the blackmail of the powerful. The Mafia trivializes these values, scorns them, tramples upon them. Because the Mafia is violence, oppression, intimidation, abuse, collusion, corruption, compromise, complicity. The Mafia is the eclipse of legality.

As long as the Mafia exists we must talk about it, discuss it, react to it. In silence criminal systems heal their wounds and reorganize, figuring out new and lethal forms of symbiosis with the economy and with political power.

Matteo Messina Denaro appears in the category of the most famous fugitives in the world. But he is not the only or the principal problem. If we stop talking about the Mafia we will pay a high price tomorrow for today's silence.

Bibliography

Ayala, Giuseppe. *Chi ha paura muore ogni giorno: i miei anni con Falcone e Borsellino*. Milan: Mondadori, 2008.

Bolzoni, Attilio. *FAQ Mafia*. Milan: Bompiani, 2010.

Bolzoni, Attilio and D'Avanzo, Giuseppe. *Il capo dei capi*. Milan: Rizzoli, 2007

Caruso, Alfio. *Da cosa nasce cosa: Storia della mafia dal 1943 a oggi*. Milan: Longanesi, 2000.

Caselli, Gian Carlo and Ingroia, Antonio. *L'eredita' scomoda. Da Falcone ad Andreotti. Sette anni a Palermo*. Milan: Feltrinelli, 2001

Dickie, John. *Cosa Nostra: A History of the Sicilian Mafia*. New York: Palgrave Macmillan, 2004.

Falcone, Giovanni, with Marcelle Padovani. *Cose di Cosa Nostra*. Milan: Rizzoli, 2004.

Fava, Claudio. *I disarmati. Storie dell'antimafia: i reduci e i complici*. Milan: Sperling and Kupfer, 2009.

Franco, Massimo. *Andreotti: la vita di un uomo politico, la storia di un'epoca*. Milan: Mondadori, 2010.

Glenny, Misha. *McMafia: A Journey Through the Global Criminal Underworld*. New York: Knopf, 2008.

Grasso, Pietro, and Francesco La Licata. *Rizzini, veleni e cicoria: la mafia prima e dopo Provenzano*. Milan: Feltrinelli, 2008.

Grasso, Pietro, and Alberto La Volpe. *Per non morire di mafia*. Milan: Sperling and Kupfer, 2009.

Ingroia, Antonio. *Nel labirinto degli dei: Storie di mafia e antimafia*. Milan: Il Saggiatore, 2010.

Lodato, Saverio. *Trent'anni di mafia: Storia di una guerra infinita*. Milan: Rizzoli, 2008.

Lodato, Saverio and Buscetta, Tommaso. *La Mafia ha vinto. Intervista con Tommaso Buscetta*. Milan: Mondadori, 2007

Lomartire, Carlo Maria. *Il bandito Giuliano: La prima storia di criminalità, politica e terrorismo nell'Italia del dopoguerra*. Milan: Mondadori, 2008.

Lucarelli, Carlo. *La mattanza: Dal silenzio sulla mafia al silenzio della mafia*. Turin: Einaudi, 2004.

Lucarelli, Carlo. *Il veleno del crimine: Storie dell'Italia oscura*. Turin: Einaudi, 2010.

Lupo, Salvatore. *Storia della Mafia: Dalle origini ai giorni nostri*. Rome: Donzelli, 2004.

Lupo, Salvatore. *Quando la mafia trovò l'America: Storia di un intreccio intercontinentale*. Turin: Einaudi, 2008.

Marino, Giuseppe Carlo. *I padrini*. Rome: Newton and Compton, 2008.

Marino, Giuseppe Carlo. *Storia della mafia*. Rome: Newton and Compton, 2009.

Palazzolo, Salvo. *I pezzi mancanti. Viaggio nei misteri della mafia*. Rome-Bari: Laterza, 2010

Palazzolo, Salvo and Prestipino, Michele. *Il codice Provenzano*. Rome-Bari: Laterza, 2009

Paoli, Letizia. *Mafia Brotherhoods*. New York: Oxford University Press, 2003.

Petacco, Arrigo. *Joe Petrosino, l'uomo che sfidò per primo la mafia italoamericana*. Milan: Mondadori, 2004.

Petacco, Arrigo. *Il prefetto di ferro. L'uomo di Mussolini che mise in ginocchio la mafia*. Milan: Mondadori, 2004

Pistone, Joseph D. *Donnie Brasco: My Undercover Life in the Mafia*. New York: New American Library, 1987.

Raab, Selwyn. *Five Families: The Rise, Decline, and Resurgence of America's Most Powerful Mafia Empires*. New York: Thomas Dunne, 2005.

Reppetto, Thomas A. *American Mafia: A History of its Rise to Power*. New York: Henry Holt, 2004.

Sifakis, Carl. *The Mafia Encyclopedia*. New York: Facts on File, 1987.

Stajano, Corrado. *Un eroe borghese*. Turin: Einaudi, 2005.

Stille, Alexander. *Excellent Cadavers*. New York: Pantheon Books, 1995.

Tranfaglia, Nicola. *Mafia, politica e affari, 1943–2008*. Rome-Bari: Laterza, 2008.

Index of names

Abbondando, Frank, 82
Accardo, Antonino Leonardo (Tony), 138, 170
Accardo, Tony. *See* Accardo, Antonino Leonardo
Adamo, Andrea, 277
Adonis, Joe, 51, 54, 82, 84, 143, 146, 150
Aglieri, Pietro, 273
Aiello, Joe. *See* Aiello, Joseph
Aiello, Joseph (Joe Aiello), 51, 54, 64
Alaimo, Dominic, 139
Alderhover, Frank, 72
Alexander, Harold, 92
Aloi, Vincenzo, 138
Altomare, Eugenio, 133
Ambrosoli, Giorgio, 179, 197
Amuso, Vittorio (Little Vic), 258
Anastasia, Albert, 51, 54, 82, 84, 91, 138, 154, 158, 160, 241
Anastasio, Umberto. *See* Anastasia, Albert
Andreotti, Giulio, 212
Angelina, Marty, 259
Aniello, Neil. *See* Migliore, Aniello
Anselmi, Albert, 61
Antinori, Ignazio, 174
Aricò, William Joseph, 197
Asbury, Herbert, 24
Badalamenti, Gaetano (Don Tano), 93, 110, 132, 178, 179, 184, 185, 193, 204, 226
Bagarella, Antonietta (Ninetta Bagarella), 189, 201
Bagarella, Calogero, 93, 121, 122, 136, 189, 201
Bagarella, Leoluca, 122, 179, 189, 191, 192, 194, 201, 229, 260, 261, 268, 275
Bagarella, Ninetta. *See* Bagarella, Antonietta
Bagarella, Salvatore, 201
Bananas, Joe. *See* Bonanno, Giuseppe
Bananas, Tony. *See* Caponigro, Antonio
Barbara, Joseph (Joe the Barber), 138
Baron, the. *See* Lo Piccolo, Salvatore
Barrile, Giovanni, 267
Basile, Emanuele, 179
Batista, Fulgenico, 139
Battaglia, Letizia, 201
Battaglia, Samuel, 170
Battaglia, Serafina, 131
Benny Eggs. *See* Mangano, Venero
Biagi, Enzo, 198, 219
Big Cheese, the. *See* DiNunzio, Carmen
Big Jim. *See* Colosimo, Giacomo

Big Paulie. *See* Castellano, Paul
Bilotti, Thomas (Tommy Bilotti), 243
Bilotti, Tommy. *See* Bilotti, Thomas
Bingham, Theodore, 36
Binu 'u Tratturi. *See* Provenzano, Bernardo
Bixio, Nino, 112
Bizzarro, Michael, 64
Blakey, G. Robert, 238
Bloody Angelo. *See* Genna, Angelo
Boccia, Ferdinand, 41
Bonanno, Giuseppe (Joe Bonanno, Joe Bananas), 51, 54, 93, 110, 138, 139, 145, 176
Bonanno, Joe. *See* Bonanno, Giuseppe
Bontate, Francesco Paolo (Don Paolino), 109
Bontate, Stefano, 109, 178, 179, 185, 202, 204, 230
Bonura, Franco, 261
Borghese, Junio Valerio, 181
Borsellino, Paolo, 8, 179, 220, 246, 260, 263, 267, 270, 280
Boss, the. *See* Masseria, Joe
Brain, the. *See* Torrio, Johnny
Brancato, Anthony, 169
Brown, Kenneth, 139
Brown, Tommy. *See* Lucchese, Gaetano
Bruno, Angelo (the Gentle Don), 154, 177, 245, 259
Brusca, Bernardo, 201, 273
Brusca, Giovanni (*Lo Scannacristiani*), 6, 7, 260, 264, 273, 275
Buchalter, Louis (Lepke), 82, 91
Bugs. *See* Moran, George Clarence
Bugsy. *See* Siegelbaum, Benjamin
Bull, the. *See* Gravano, Sammy
Bundesen, Herman N., 69
Buscetta, Tommaso (Don Masino), 6, 8, 10, 93, 110, 134, 178, 179, 185, 189, 213, 215, 220, 221, 222, 260, 267
Byrnes, Thomas F., 24, 25
Calderone, Pippo, 178, 179
Calì, Francesco Paolo (Franky Boy, Frank Calì), 252, 261
Calì, Frank. *See* Calì, Francesco Paolo Calì
Calò, Giuseppe (Pippo Calò), 189, 197, 201, 229, 330
Calò, Pippo. *See* Calò, Giuseppe
Calvi, Roberto, 197, 230
Capa, Robert, 94
Capitano Ultimo. *See* De Caprio, Sergio

Capone, Al. *See* Capone, Alphonse Gabriel
Capone, Albert Francis (Sonny Capone), 71
Capone, Alphonse Gabriel (Al Capone, Scarface), 27, 51, 52, 54, 60, 61, 64, 67, 70, 71, 72, 74, 79, 80, 170, 245, 251
Capone, Matthew, 72
Capone, Sonny. *See* Capone, Albert Francis
Caponigro, Antonio (Tony Bananas), 177
Caponnetto, Antonino, 208, 220, 221
Capraro, Vincenzo, 16
Carbo, Frankie. *See.* Carbo, Paolo Giovanni
Carbo, Paolo Giovanni (Frankie Carbo, Mr. Fury), 82, 152
Carboni, Flavio, 197
Carnevale, Salvatore (Turiddu Carnevale), 129, 130
Carnevale, Turiddu. *See* Carnevale, Salvatore
Carollo, Anthony, 240
Carollo, Silvestro (Silver Dollar Sam), 175
Caruso, Enrico, 15, 24
Casamento, Filippo, 261
Cascio Ferro, Vito, 25, 35, 36, 38, 40, 41, 43, 54
Cassarà, Ninni, 179, 208, 219, 221, 267
Castellano, Giuseppe, 154
Castellano, Paul (Big Paulie), 139, 154, 155, 157, 241, 243, 251
Castiglia, Francesco (Frank Costello), 51, 54, 57, 84, 138, 141, 146, 150, 174, 244
Castro, Fidel, 174
Castrogiovanni, Giovanni, 17
Catalano, Agostino, 267
Cavataio, Michele (the Cobra), 93, 134, 136
Charles of Anjou, 14
Chemist, the. *See* Marino Mannoia, Francesco
Chin, the. *See* Gigante, Vincent
Chinnici, Rocco, 179, 208, 219, 220, 267, 273
Ciacci, Giorgio, 133
Ciaccio Montalto, Giangiacomo, 179
Ciancimino, Vito Alfio, 181, 213, 215
Ciaschiteddu. *See* Salvatore Greco
Cinà, Antonino, 261
Cirillo, Alphonse, 257
Cirillo, Dominick (the Quiet Dom), 257
Clark, James, 67
Cobra, the. *See* Cavataio, Michele
Coen Luzzato, Irene, 89
Cohen, Mickey, 72, 84, 167
Coll, Vincent (Mad Dog), 56

Colombo, Joe. *See* Colombo, Joseph
Colombo, Joseph (Joe Colombo), 138, 154, 161, 162, 258
Colosimo, Giacomo (Big Jim), 51, 60, 64
Contorno, Salvatore (Totuccio), 221
Coppola, Francesco (Frank Three Fingers), 119
Corallo, Anthony, 138
Corbo, Rosalia, 232
Corozzo, Joseph, 254
Corozzo, Nicholas (Little Nick), 255, 256, 261
Corrao, Silvio, 133
Corso, Gioacchino, 254, 261
Corso, Gianpaolo, 261
Cosina, Walter, 267
Costa, Filippo, 191
Costa, Gaetano, 179
Costello, Frank. *See* Castiglia, Francesco
Coughlin, Mary, 71
Crane, Cheryl, 168
Crazy Joe Gallo. *See* Gallo, Joe
Crea, Steven (Wonderboy), 239
Crispi, Francesco, 11, 23, 112
Croswell, Edgar, 138, 139
Cucco, Alfredo, 41, 47
D'Alfonso, Frank, 259
D'Amico, John (Jackie the Nose), 255, 256
Dalla Chiesa, Carlo Alberto, 9, 179, 211, 263, 280
Dapper Don, the. *See* Gotti, John Joseph
De Caprio, Sergio (Capitano Ultimo), 237
DeCavalcante, Sam. *See* DeCavalcante, Simone
DeCavalcante, Simone (Decavalcante, Sam), 170
DeCicco, Joe, 256
Dee, Joey. *See* DiNapoli, Joseph
De Felice Giuffrida, Giuseppe, 11
De Gennaro, Gianni, 220, 221
Dellacroce, Aniello (Neal Dellacroce), 241, 243
Dellacroce, Neal. *See* Dellacroce, Aniello
De Mauro, Mauro, 182
De Mauro, Tullio, 182
DeStefano, Sam, 172
Dewey, Thomas E., 83, 90, 141
Dicillo, Rocco, 264
Dickens, Charles, 31
Di Cristina, Giuseppe (the Tiger), 178
Di Girolamo, Mario, 93
Di Lello, Giuseppe, 220, 267
Dillinger, John, 66
Di Maria, Emanuele, 126
Di Maria, Gregorio, 104, 106
Di Matteo, Giuseppe, 9, 229, 272, 273, 278
Di Matteo, Santino, 272
DiNapoli, Joseph (Joey Dee), 258
DiNunzio, Carmen (the Big Cheese), 259
Diotallevi, Ernesto, 197

Di Pisa, Calcedonio, 93, 122
Di Salvo, Rosario, 206
Di Stefano, Frankie, 254
Don Calò. *See* Vizzini, Calogero
Don Ciccio. *See* Messina Denaro, Francesco
Don Masino. *See* Buscetta, Tommaso
Don Paolino. *See* Bontade, Francesco Paolo
Don Tano. *See* Badalamenti, Gaetano
Doto, Giuseppe Antonio, 143
Dragna, Jack, 84, 169
Drucci, Vincent, 77
Dukakis, Michael, 59
Dürig, Ernst, 44
Eastman, Monk, 27
Eboli, Thomas ("Tommy Ryan"), 146, 148, 154, 257
Enforcer, the. *See* Nitti, Frank
Epstein, Joe, 88
Evola, Natale, 138
Falcone, Giovanni, 7, 8, 9, 10, 179, 189, 208, 220, 221, 222, 225, 229, 246, 260, 263, 264, 267, 270, 273, 280
Fanelli, Rocco, 72
Fardelli, Marino, 133
Fat Tony. *See* Salemo, Anthony
Fava, Giuseppe (Pippo Fava), 179, 219
Fava, Pippo. *See* Fava, Giuseppe
Ferrara, Eric, 6, 7
Fidanzati, Gaetano, 278
Filippello, Matteo, 43
Finocchiaro Aprile, Andrea, 108, 109
Flaccomio, Antonio, 24, 25
Flegenheimer, Arthur Simon (Dutch Schultz), 54, 83, 90
Flusser, Vilèm, 9
Fontana, Giuseppe, 43
Fox, the. *See* Torrio, Johnny
Francese, Mario, 131, 179, 194
Franchetti, Leopoldo, 10, 19
Frangiamore, Samuel (Sam the Farmer), 176
Frank Three Fingers. *See* Coppola, Francesco
Fratiano, Jimmy, 169
Gagliano, Gaetano, 152
Gagliano, Tommy, 138
Galante, Carmine (Lilo), 49, 93, 110, 138, 139, 145, 248
Galatolo, Angelo, 129
Galatolo, Gaetano, 129
Gallo, Joe (Crazy Joe), 155, 161, 162, 258
Gallo, Larry, 162
Galluccio, Frank, 70
Gambino, Carlo, 51, 138, 139, 145, 148, 152, 154, 155, 157, 158, 161, 204, 241
Gambino, Emanuel, 156
Garibaldi, Giuseppe, 11, 18, 122
Gelli, Licio, 230
Genna, Angelo (Bloody Angelo), 77
Genovese, Vito, 41, 49, 51, 54, 84, 94, 96,

138, 141, 145, 146, 148, 150, 154
Gentle Don, the. *See* Bruno, Angelo
Geraci, Antonino, 201
Giancana, Salvatore (Sam), 138, 139, 170, 174
Gigante, Salvatore, 244
Gigante, Vincent (the Chin), 51, 150, 240, 244, 246, 257
Gigante, Yolanda, 244
Gillis, Lester Joseph (Baby Face Nelson), 66
Giufrè, Antonino, 270
Giuliani, Rudolph, 239, 243, 246
Giuliano, Alessandro, 192
Giuliano, Boris, 179, 192, 229
Giuliano, Salvatore (Turiddu), 92, 96, 98, 99, 102, 104, 106,107, 126, 132
Gotti, John Angelo III ("Junior" Gotti), 256
Gotti, John Joseph (the Dapper Don, the Teflon Don), 6, 7, 157, 238, 240, 243, 244, 251, 255, 256
Gotti, Peter (One-Eyed Pete), 255
Granta, Ursula Sue, 80
Grassi, Libero, 235
Grasso, Pietro, 220
Gravano, Salvatore (Sammy the Bull), 251, 255
Graviano, Filippo, 268, 270
Graviano, Giuseppe, 268, 270
Graviano, Michele, 270
Greco, Giuseppe, 184
Greco, Michele (the Pope), 8, 178, 184, 185, 194, 201, 215, 226
Greco, Pino (*Scarpuzzedda*), 179, 187, 191, 204, 208, 253
Greco, Salvatore (*Ciaschiteddu*), 93, 110, 123, 132, 178
Grigoli, Salvatore, 268
Gualterio, Filippo Antonio, 10
Guarnotta, Leonardo, 220, 267
Gusenberg, Peter, 67
Harnett, Gabby, 71
Hayez, Francesco, 14
Hennessey, David, 26
Heyer, Adam, 67
Hill, Virginia, 88
Hoffa, James Riddle (Jimmy), 176
Hoover, J. Edgar, 7, 66, 139, 155
Huston, Arthur, 139
Iceman, the. *See* Kuklinski, Richard
Ida, Joseph, 177, 245
Immortal, the. *See* Persico, Carmine
Impastato, Giuseppe (Peppino Impastato), 179, 185, 193
Impastato, Peppino. *See* Impastato, Giuseppe
Indelicato, Alphonse (Sonny Red), 248
Insalco, Giuseppe, 179
Inzerillo, Antonino, 276
Inzerillo, Giovanni, 253, 261

Inzerillo, Giuseppe, 253
Inzerillo, Pietro, 276
Inzerillo, Pietro (Tall Pete), 253
Inzerillo, Rosario, 276
Inzerillo, Salvatore (Totuccio Inzerillo), 132, 178, 179, 204, 253, 261, 276
Inzerillo, Tommaso, 276
Inzerillo, Totuccio. See Inzerillo, Salvatore
Ioele, Francesco. See Yale, Frankie
Jackie the Nose. See D'Amico, John
Jacovelli, Joseph, 162
Joe the Barber. See Barbara, Joseph
John the Eagle. See Riggi, Giovanni
Jordan, Don, 152
Junior Gotti. See Gotti, John Angelo III
Kefauver, Estes, 88, 150
Kelly, Paul. See Vaccarelli, Antonio
Kennedy, John Fitzgerald, 138, 170, 174
Kennedy, Robert, 138, 139, 170
Krieger, Albert, 145
Kuklinski, Richard (the Iceman), 248
La Barbera, Angelo, 93, 110, 122, 123, 132, 134, 189
La Barbera, Girolamo, 278
La Barbera, Salvatore, 93, 122, 123, 132, 134
La Guardia, Achille, 89
LaGuardia, Fiorello, 83, 90, 175, 246
Lansky, Meyer, 27, 56, 57, 58, 83, 84, 140, 150, 158
La Pira, Giorgio, 202
La Torre, Pio, 179, 202, 206, 208
Leale, Salvatore, 131
Leale, Stefano, 131
Leggio, Luciano. See Liggio, Luciano
Leone, Antonino, 17
Letizia, Calogero, 17
Letizia, Giuseppe, 116
Li Causi, Girolamo, 100
Ligambi, Joseph Anthony (Uncle Joe), 259
Liggio, Luciano (Luciano Leggio, Lucianeddu), 93, 116, 119, 121, 122, 123, 182, 185, 201
Liggio, Nando, 237
Lima, Salvatore Achille Ettore (Salvo Lima), 181, 212, 213, 221, 237
Lima, Salvo. See Lima, Salvatore Achille Ettore
Li Muli, Vincenzo, 267
Linares, Vincenzo, 13
Lipari, Vito, 179
Lissoni, Igea, 142
Little Nick. See Corozzo, Nicholas
Little Nicky. See Scarfo, Nicodemo Domenico
Little Vic. See Amuso, Vittorio
Livatino, Rosario, 232
Livatino, Vincenzo, 232
Li Vecchi, Alfredo, 237
LoCascio, Salvatore, 239
Loi, Emanuela, 267

Lombardo, Antonio, 64
Lo Piccolo, Salvatore (the Baron), 261, 277, 278
Lo Piccolo, Sandro, 277
Lo Russo, Antonino, 182
Louis VIII, king of France, 14
Louis-Philippe-Robert, duke of Orléans, 21
Lovett, Bill (Wild Bill), 61
Lo Voi, Gioacchino, 42
Luca, Ugo, 102, 106, 211
Lucania, Salvatore (Lucky Luciano), 6, 7, 41, 51, 54, 56, 58, 84, 90, 93, 94, 96, 109, 110, 141, 142, 143, 146, 148, 150, 155, 161, 176, 238, 258
Lucchese, Gaetano (Tommy Brown, Tommy Lucchese), 138, 139, 152, 154, 161
Lucchese, Tommy. See Lucchese, Gaetano
Luciano, Lucky. See Lucania, Salvatore
Macheca, Joseph, 26
McClellan, John, 238
McGurn, Jack (Machine Gun), 72
Mad Butcher, the, 74
Mad Dog. See Coll, Vincent
Mad Hatter. See Anastasia, Albert
Madonia, Benedetto, 25, 38
Madonia, Francesco, 201
Madonia, Nino, 194
Madonna, Matt. See Madonna, Matthew
Madonna, Matthew (Matt Madonnna), 258
Magaddino, Stefano, 51, 54, 138, 139, 154, 176
Magliocco, Joseph, 138, 161, 257
Malausa, Mario, 133
Malone, Harry, 82
Mancuso, Lenin, 201
Mandalà, Nicola, 252
Mangano, Venero (Benny Eggs), 257
Mangano, Vincent, 61, 138, 154, 257
Manno, Salvatore, 93
Manzella, Cesare, 93, 193
Maranzano, Salvatore, 40, 51, 54, 56, 83, 96, 149
Marcello, Carlos, 175
Marcinkus, Paul Casimir, 198
Marino Mannoia, Francesco (Mozzarella, the Chemist), 198, 230, 260
Mascagni, Pietro, 15
Masseria, Joe (the Boss), 51, 54, 56, 57, 84, 96, 143, 149
Massimo, Joe, 257
Matranga, Antonino, 93
Matranga, Charlie, 26
Mattarella, Bernardo, 202
Mattarella, Piersanti, 179, 202, 206
Mattarella, Sergio, 202
Mattei, Enrico, 182
Matteotti, Giacomo, 44, 235
May, John, 67

Medeiros, Celestino, 59
Meli, Antonino, 221
Merlino, Joseph, 259
Merlo, Mike, 61
Messina Denaro, Francesco (Don Ciccio), 280
Messina Denaro, Matteo ('u Siccu), 261, 277, 280, 281
Migliore, Aniello (Neil Aniello), 258
Milazzo, Silvio, 112
Milillo, Ignazio, 121
Mr. Fury. See Carbo, Paolo Giovanni
Moncada, Girolamo, 136
Monroe, Marilyn, 138, 170
Montagna, Salvatore (Sal the Iron Worker), 257
Montalto Ciaccio, Giangiacomo, 215
Montana, Beppe. See Montana, Giuseppe
Montana, Giuseppe (Beppe Montana), 179, 219, 221, 267
Montgomery, Bernard Law, 92
Montinaro, Antonio, 264
Monzello, Jack, 64
Moran, Bugs. See Moran, George Clarence
Moran, George Clarence (Bugs), 67, 72, 77
Morelli, Butsey, 59
Morello, Giuseppe (Pidu Morello), 25, 35, 54, 150
Moretti, Guarino (Willie), 146
Mori, Cesare, 41, 43, 44, 45, 46, 47, 97, 211
Mori, Mario, 237
Morvillo, Francesca Laura, 264
Mosca, Gaetano, 6, 10
Motisi, Lorenzo, 93
Mussolini, Benito, 40, 44, 49, 96, 97, 235
Mutolo, Gaspare, 192
Napoli, Gaetano, 254
Napoli, Thomas, 254
Natoli, Luigi, 13
Navarra, Michele, 93, 116, 119, 122
Navetta, Francesco, 17
Nelson, Baby Face. See Gillis, Lester Joseph
Ness, Eliot, 74
Nicchi, Gianni. See Nicchi, Giovanni
Nicchi, Giovanni (Nicchi, Gianni), 252, 261, 278
Nitti, Frank (Francesco Raffaele Nitto; the Enforcer), 80, 81, 170
Nitto, Francesco Raffaele. See Nitti, Frank
Noe, Joe, 83
Notarbartolo, Emanuele, 40, 42, 182
Nuccio, Pasquale, 133
O'Banion, Dion, 61, 64, 67, 77
O'Dwyer, William, 82
O'Hare, Edward Henry "Butch," 79
O'Hare, Edward Joseph, 79, 80
One-Eyed Pete. See Gotti, Peter
Oswald, Lee Harvey, 174
Ox, the. See Petto, Thomas

Palizzolo, Raffaele, 40, 43
Panno, Giuseppe, 93
Parisi, Roberto, 217
Passatempo, Giovanni, 126
Patri Nostru. *See* Navarra, Michele
Patti, Gaia, 217
Patti, Piero, 179, 217
Patton, George S., 92
Pecoraro, Salvatore, 102
Persico, Carmine (the Snake; the Immortal), 6,
    138, 162, 240, 258
Petrosino, Joe, 25, 35, 36, 38
Petto, Thomas (the Ox), 38
Picciutteddu. *See* Nicchi, Giovanni
Piddu Morello. *See* Morello, Giuseppe
Pisanu, Giuseppe, 136
Pisciotta, Gaspare, 101, 106, 107, 126
Pitré, Giuseppe, 6
Polazzi, Antonio, 24
Poletti, Charles, 92, 94
Profaci, Giuseppe (Joe Profaci), 51, 54, 138,
    139, 161, 162, 258
Profaci, Joe. *See* Profaci, Giuseppe
Provenzano, Bernardo (*Binu 'u Tratturi*), 6, 7,
    93, 121, 122, 136, 178, 189, 191, 194, 201,
    215, 222, 229, 260, 261, 275, 277, 278, 280
Provenzano, Joe, 26
Puglisi, Giuseppe, 268, 270
Pulizzi, Gaspare, 277
Quarteraro, Carlo, 24, 25
Quarteraro, Vincenzo, 24, 25
Quiet Don, the. *See* Gotti, John Joseph
Raccuglia, Domenico, 278
Reina, Michele, 179
Reles, Abe, 79
Ricca, Paul, 170
Riccobono, Rosario, 187
Riggi, Giovanni (John the Eagle), 170
Riina, Francesco, 121
Riina, Salvatore (*Totò 'u Curtu*), 7, 93, 121,
    122, 136, 178, 179, 182, 189, 191, 192,
    194, 201, 204, 206, 215, 222, 229, 237,
    260, 261, 263, 275
Riis, Jacob, 30, 31
Rimi, Filippo, 131
Rimi, Vincenzo, 131
Rinaldi, Placido, 17
Rizzotto, Giuseppe, 6, 10
Rizzotto, Placido, 93, 116, 119, 211
Robinson, Edward G., 238
Rodd, Francis, 92
Roosevelt, Franklin Delano, 66, 90
Roosevelt, Theodore, 25, 36
Rosen, Joseph, 91
Rotolo, Antonio (Nino Rotolo), 261, 278
Rotolo, Nino. *See* Rotolo, Antonio
Rubinello, Joseph, 64
Ruby, Jack, 174

Russo, Domenico, 211
Russo, Giovanni, 116
Russo, Giuseppe, 191, 194
Russo, Giuseppe Genco, 92, 93, 109, 110,
    112, 122
Russo, Joseph, 64
Sacco, Nicola, 59
Saetta, Antonino, 179
Sage, Walter, 79
Saietta, Ignazio (the Wolf), 25, 34
Salerno, Anthony (Fat Tony), 246, 251
Salerno, Tony. *See* Salemo, Anthony
Salomone, Antonino, 93
Sal the Iron Worker. *See* Montagna,
    Salvatore
Salvo, Ignazio, 220, 221, 225, 237
Salvo, Nino, 220, 225
Sam the Farmer. *See* Frangiamore, Samuel
Santapaola, Nitto, 178, 219
Scaglione, Pietro, 182, 211
Scalice, Francesco (Frank Scalice), 61, 160
Scalice, Frank. *See* Scalice, Francesco
Scalice, Joseph, 160
Scarface. *See* Capone, Alphonse Gabriel
Scarfo, Nicodemo Domenico (Little Nicky),
    245, 259
Scelba, Mario, 126
Schifani, Vito, 264
Schiro, Cola, 40
Schirò, Giacomo, 100
Schultz, Dutch. *See* Flegenheimer, Arthur
    Simon
Schwimmer, Reinhardt, 67
Sciacca, Paul, 138
Scopelliti, Antonio, 272
Scorsese, Martin, 24
Seagal, Steven, 255
Serio, Francesca, 130
Setti Carraro, Emanuela, 211
Settineri, Roberto, 254, 261
Sica, Domenico, 221
Siccu. *See* Messina Denaro, Matteo
Siegel, Bugsy, 27, 54, 56, 57, 83, 88, 141,
    150, 167
Siegelbaum, Benjamin. *See* Siegel, Bugsy
Signurinu. *See* Aglieri, Pietro
Silver Dollar Sam. *See* Carollo, Silvestro
Sinatra, Frank (Francis Albert), 155
Sindona, Michele, 197, 198, 230
Snake, the. *See* Persico, Carmine
Sonnino, Sidney, 10, 19
Sonny Red. *See* Indelicato, Alphonse
Socri, Francesco, 93
Spatuzza, Gaspare, 268, 270
Stompanato, Johnny, 167, 168
Straus, Harry, 82
Strollo, Anthony, 146
Suchowljanski, Majer. *See* Lanksy, Meyer

Tall Pete. *See* Inzerillo, Pietro
Teflon Don, the. *See* Gotti, John Joseph
Teresa, Vincent, 59
Terranova, Antonio, 25
Terranova, Cesare, 132, 179, 201, 220
Terranova, Ciro, 25, 83, 150
Terranova, Francesco, 132
Terranova, Vincenzo, 25
Tieri, Frank, 148
Tiger, the. *See* Di Cristina, Giuseppe
Tommy Brown. *See* Lucchese, Gaetano
Tommy Ryan. *See* Eboli, Thomas
Tommy Three Fingers. *See* Lucchese, Gaetano
Torretta, Pietro, 132, 189
Torrio, Johnny (the Brain, the Fox), 6, 27, 60,
    61, 64, 74, 77
Totò 'u Curtu. *See* Riina, Salvatore
Trafficante, Santo, Jr.,174
Trafficante, Santo, Sr., 174
Traina, Claudio, 267
Tramunti, Carmine, 138, 152, 258
Tresca, Carlo, 49, 145
Troina, Marino, 93
Trombino, Anthony, 169
Truman, Harry S., 90
Turiddu. *See* Giuliano, Salvatore
Turner, Lana, 168
Ulloa Calà, Pietro, 10
Uncle Joe. *See* Ligambi, Joseph Anthony
Vaccarelli, Antonio (Paul Kelly), 27, 64
Vaccaro, Calogero, 133
Valachi, Joe, 146, 149
Vanzetti, Bartolomeo, 59
Vasisko, Vincent, 138, 139
Venturi, Vincenzo, 17
Verga, Giovanni, 15, 21
Verro, Bernardino, 11, 23, 122
Victor Emmanuel III, king of Italy, 11
Vidocq, Eugène François, 24
Villabianca, Francesco Maria Emanuele e
    Gaetani, marchese of, 13
Vitale, Leonardo, 215, 230
Vizzini, Calogero (Don Calò, 'u zu Calò), 41,
    92, 93, 94, 97, 99, 109, 110, 122, 124, 202
Volstead, Andrew John, 50, 51, 52
Weinshank, Albert, 67
Weiss, Earl, 77
Wild Bill. *See* Lovett, Bill
Willie. *See* Moretti, Guarino
Winter, Dale, 60
Wolf, the. *See* Saietta, Ignazio
Wonderboy. *See* Crea, Steven
Yale, Frankie, 27, 60, 61, 62, 63, 143
Yale, Lucy, 62
Zicari, Emanuel, 139
Zu Calò. *See* Vizzini, Calogero
Zu Peppi Genco. *See* Russo, Giuseppe Genco
Zu Tanu. *See* Galatolo, Gaetano

Photo References

Abbreviations:
a = above; b = below; r = right; l = left

Agenzia Fotogramma, Milan: Aldo Cavaliere, 197b; / Giacominofoto: 116–117; Letizia Battaglia, 201; Franco Caramanna, 232; Alessandro Fucarini, 228; Agenzia Fotografica Labruzzo, 192, 195, 203, 227; Filippo Lacava, 226; Santi Caleca, 135; Studio Camera, 184, 254a, 262, 266; Studio Camera / Lannino & Naccari, 253b, 274, 276

AKG-Images, Berlin: 14, 15, 32

Alinari Archives, Florence: Eugenio Interguglielmi, 20–21; The Granger Collection, New York, 43, 58, 96a, 150

C.I.D.M.A., Corleone: 23

© Contrasto, Milan: Cornella Capa Photos / Robert Capa, 94

© Corbis Italia, Milan: ANSA, 211b, 277b; Bettmann, 27, 28–29, 30, 31, 33, 34, 47, 52, 53, 54, 55, 56, 57, 59, 60, 61, 62, 63, 64, 66, 65, 71, 72, 73, 74, 75, 76, 77, 78, 79, 80, 81, 82, 83b, 84, 86–87, 88, 89, 91, 141, 142, 143, 144, 145, 146, 147, 148, 149, 151, 152, 153, 154, 156–157, 158–159, 160, 161, 162, 163, 167, 168, 169, 170, 171, 172–173, 174, 175, 176, 177, 185, 244, 248, 249, 251; Hulton-Deutsch Collection, 48–49, 67, 72, 90; Lannino-Naccari, 277a, 279, 281; Robert Maass, 247; Mike Palazzotto, 278; / Sygma: JP Laffont, 246; Rick Maiman, 256a; Jeffrey Markowitz, 250; Franco Origlia, 200–201

Fototeca Storica Nazionale Ando Gilardi, Milan: 17, 22, 35, 37, 42, 44, 100

© Getty Images, Milan: Slim Aarons, 140; Marianne Barcellona, 240; Chicago History Museum, 68–69, 70; Ed Clark, 166; Yvonne Hemsey, 258a; New York Daily News, 38, 241, 242–243, 255

© Olycom, Milan: 101, 210, CGE, 268; Mercurio, 275; Mike Palazzotto, 193, 264, 270, 272, 275; Studio Camera, 252, 253a

Photoservice Electa, Milan: 18; / Mondadori Vintage Collection, 26, 36, 45, 85, 95, 104–105, 106, 132l, 155a, 164, 165, 198, 199, 205, 206–207, 208, 209, 211a, 212a, 214, 223, 229, 245

© Photoshot, London: 83a, 155b, 196, 197a

Pubblifoto, Palermo / Enzo Brai: 12, 13, 16, 46, 96b, 98, 99, 102, 103, 104, 107, 108, 109, 110, 111, 112, 113, 114–115, 116, 118, 119, 120, 121, 124, 125, 126, 126–127, 128, 129, 130, 131, 132r, 133, 134, 136, 137, 180–181, 182, 183, 186, 187, 188, 189, 190–191, 194, 202, 204, 212b, 213, 215, 216–217, 218, 219, 222, 224, 225, 230, 231, 233, 234–235, 236, 237, 263, 265, 267, 269, 271, 273

The Library of Congress, Washington, DC: 29; Grantham Bain Collection, 19l

The publisher wishes to thank Enzo Brai for his invaluable contribution to the photo research. Thanks also to the Sidney Sonnino Archive at the University of Siena, the Archivio Storico of the Senate of the Italian Republic, the Centro Internazionale di Documentazione sulle Mafie e Movimento Antimafia of Corleone.

Art director Dario Tagliabue

Editorial director Lidia Maurizi

Graphic coordination Lucia Vigo

Graphic design Sara De Michele

Layouts Giorgia Dalla Pietà

Illustration coordination Elisa Dal Canto

Picture research Silvia Piombo

Technical coordination Rosella Lazzarotto

Quality control Giancarlo Berti

English-language translation Jay Hyams

English-language typesetting Michael Shaw